1996
HAUT-MÉDOC
CRU CLASSÉ EN 1868

INDOOR *edible* GARDEN

ZIA ALLAWAY

Project Editor Susannah Steel
Senior Art Editors Sonia Moore, Alison Gardner
Designer Rehan Abdul
Editorial assistant Alice Horne
Senior Jackets Creative Nicky Powling
Producer (Pre-production) Catherine Williams
Senior Producer Ché Creasey
Creative Technical Support Sonia Charbonnier
Managing Editors Dawn Henderson, Angela Wilkes
Managing Art Editor Marianne Markham
Art Director Maxine Pedliham
Publishing Director Mary-Clare Jerram

First published in Great Britain in 2017
by Dorling Kindersley Limited
80 Strand, London WC2R 0RL

A Penguin Random House Company

2 4 6 8 10 9 7 5 3 1
001–291141–Mar/2017

A CIP catalogue record for this book is
available from the British Library.

ISBN 978-0-2412-4897-3

Printed and bound in China

A WORLD OF IDEAS:
SEE ALL THERE IS TO KNOW

www.dk.com

Contents

Try a taster first
When you try something new, there is a possibility that you may be allergic to it or simply not like the flavour, so before growing a crop that you then can't eat, buy a taster from a shop first. If you are pregnant or suffer from an ailment, contact your GP before trying a new herb or fruit.

Introduction 12

Planning an indoor edible garden 14

Where to grow your edibles 16
Bright sunlit zones 18
Partially sunlit zones 20
Cool zones 22
Best indoor edibles 24
Choosing a container 28
Types of container 30

Herbs & edible flowers 32

Introducing herbs & edible flowers 34
Herbs & edible flowers in pots for a windowsill 36
Thyme 40
Scented geranium & herb windowbox 42
Basil 46
Grow your own herbal teas 48
Edible orchids mounted onto bark 52
Edible flowers 56
Edible flower ladder 58
Grow lemongrass from shop-bought stems 60
Cocktail herbs & fruits 62
Mint 66
Herbs in hanging jars 68
Oregano & parsley 72
Sage & rosemary 74

Continued »

Sprouts, leaves & roots 76

Introducing sprouts, leaves & roots 78

Sprouts in jars 80
Sprouts 82
Microgreens in muffin cases 84
Microgreens 88
Transform your shelves into a mini greenhouse 90
Salad leaves 96
Table-top spicy leaves 98
Tangy garlic shoots 102
Chives & spring onions 104
Pots of tasty roots 106
Radishes 110
Pots of crunchy carrots 112
Carrots 116
Oyster mushrooms in 14 days 118
Mushrooms 120

Fruiting vegetables 122

Introducing fruiting vegetables 124

Chilli & herb ball 126
Chilli peppers 130
Mediterranean mix 132
Aubergines 136
Tiny tomatoes in a colander 138
Tomatoes 142
Tomato towers 144
Tamarillo tree tomatoes 146
Cucumbers on wheels 148
Cucumbers 154
Cucamelons in hanging crates 156
Raise sweet peppers in colourful pots 160
Sweet peppers 162

5

Fruit 164

Introducing fruit 166

Wild strawberry shelves 168
Strawberries 172
Fruit & flower windowbox 174
Grow your own curry leaves 176
Lemons & limes 178
Oranges in pots for a sunny room 180
Oranges 184
Fruity fig tree 186
Peaches & nectarines 190
Pineapple guavas 192
Cape gooseberries 194

6

Expert's tips 196

Planning your indoor edible gardening year 198
Choosing the right compost 200
Watering & feeding indoor edibles 202
Sowing from seed 204
Pruning, training, & pollinating fruit crops 206
Common pests & diseases 208
Preserving your harvests 210
Useful resources 212
Index 214
Acknowledgements 221

Introduction

Whether you live in an **apartment** with **no outdoor space**, or simply want to try a few tender crops, this book opens up a world of possibilities for **growing your own food indoors**. Most of the projects are very easy, too, so you will need no previous experience if you want to enjoy your own freshly picked produce.

Nothing beats the fresh taste of a just-picked tomato or lettuces that are harvested minutes before eating, and simple delights like these can be within easy reach if you care for just a few crops in pots inside your home. Packed with projects, this book shows you how to grow everything from herbs on a windowsill to aubergines in a sunny dining room, and each has a level of difficulty to help you choose what's right for you. It also provides all the information and growing advice you'll need to raise a wide range of delicious crops successfully indoors.

Just remember that unlike other projects in the home, such as decorating or cooking, all gardening projects require some aftercare, so you need to assess how much time you will have to nurture your treasures. If you have a busy schedule, choose crops that will cope with less watering and feeding, such as herbs or edible flowers. Also, experiment and have fun trying new things; part of the joy of growing your own is simply having a go. You may be surprised at what you can achieve – and which plants will thrive happily indoors. As well as growing staples such as salad leaves, strawberries, and tomatoes, why not include an exotic crop or two; Cape gooseberries produce small fruits inside papery cases with little fuss, while citrus trees can fruit successfully given the right conditions.

Research shows that gardening, whether it is indoors or outside, improves the health of both mind and body, and although you won't be exerting yourself by digging a border, you will feel the benefits of growing a plant from seed or enjoying the jewel-like colours of fruits as they form. Guaranteed to reduce stress, calm the nerves, and rest your eyes from an ever-present screen, growing your own food is one of the best therapies for a modern lifestyle. So now all you have to do is turn the page and start growing!

Zia Allaway

Planning an indoor edible garden

Find out how much space and sunlight you will need to create a mini productive garden inside your home, and explore the range of beautiful pots and containers you can use to accommodate your homegrown crops.

Where to grow your edibles

Whatever the size of your home, there is a selection of edible plants you can grow indoors, as long as you have some **natural daylight** filtering in. The areas, or "**zones**" where plants will grow can be **windowsills,** beneath a **skylight**, in **bright rooms**, and even in a **dark**, unlit area if you install grow lights.

Bright sunlit zones

These zones, which include south-facing rooms, areas by large west- or east-facing windows and below skylights, suit the widest range of plants. They offer the maximum amount of natural sunlight for much of the day, especially during spring and summer.

SOUTH-FACING WINDOWS

OTHER WINDOWS

Zone 3

BENEATH A SKYLIGHT

Partially sunlit zones

For rooms with windows facing east or west, choose crops such as lettuces that tolerate partial shade. Sun-loving plants may produce fruit on windowsills, but not as much as in a bright area. In gloomy sites such as north-facing rooms, grow lights will aid productivity.

WALLS

DARK CORNERS

Zone 6

CENTRE OF A ROOM

Cool zones

Outside windowsills and unheated rooms are useful for crops such as fruit trees that, in their native habitat, have a dormant winter period and plants with flowers normally pollinated by insects.

COOL, SOUTH-FACING ROOM

OUTSIDE WINDOWSILL

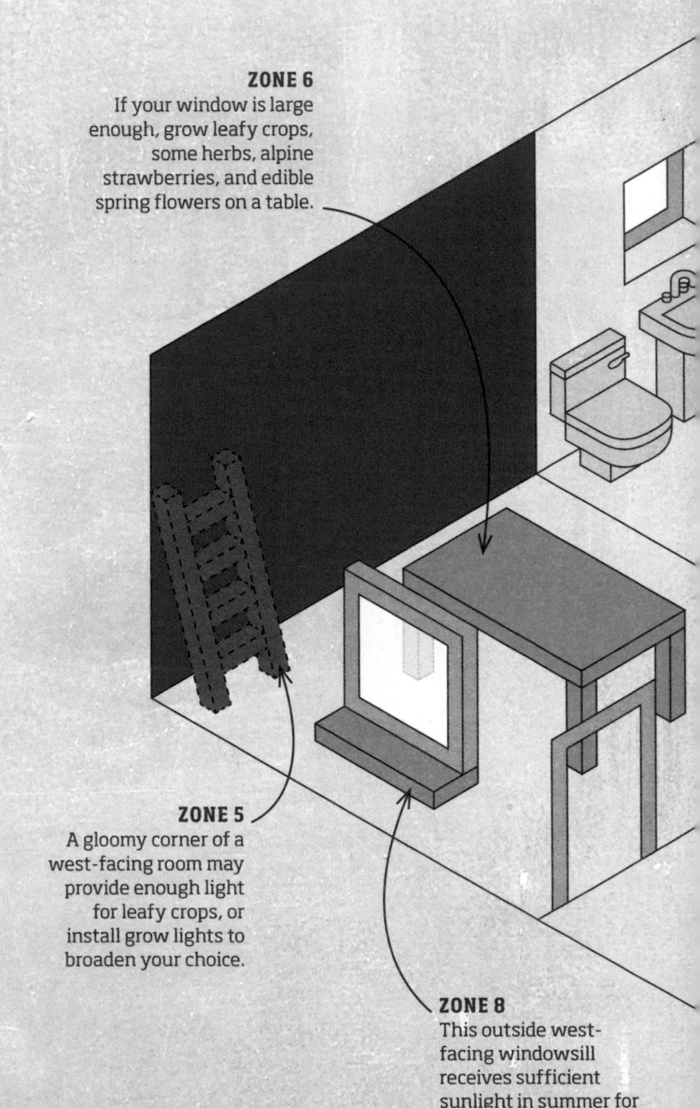

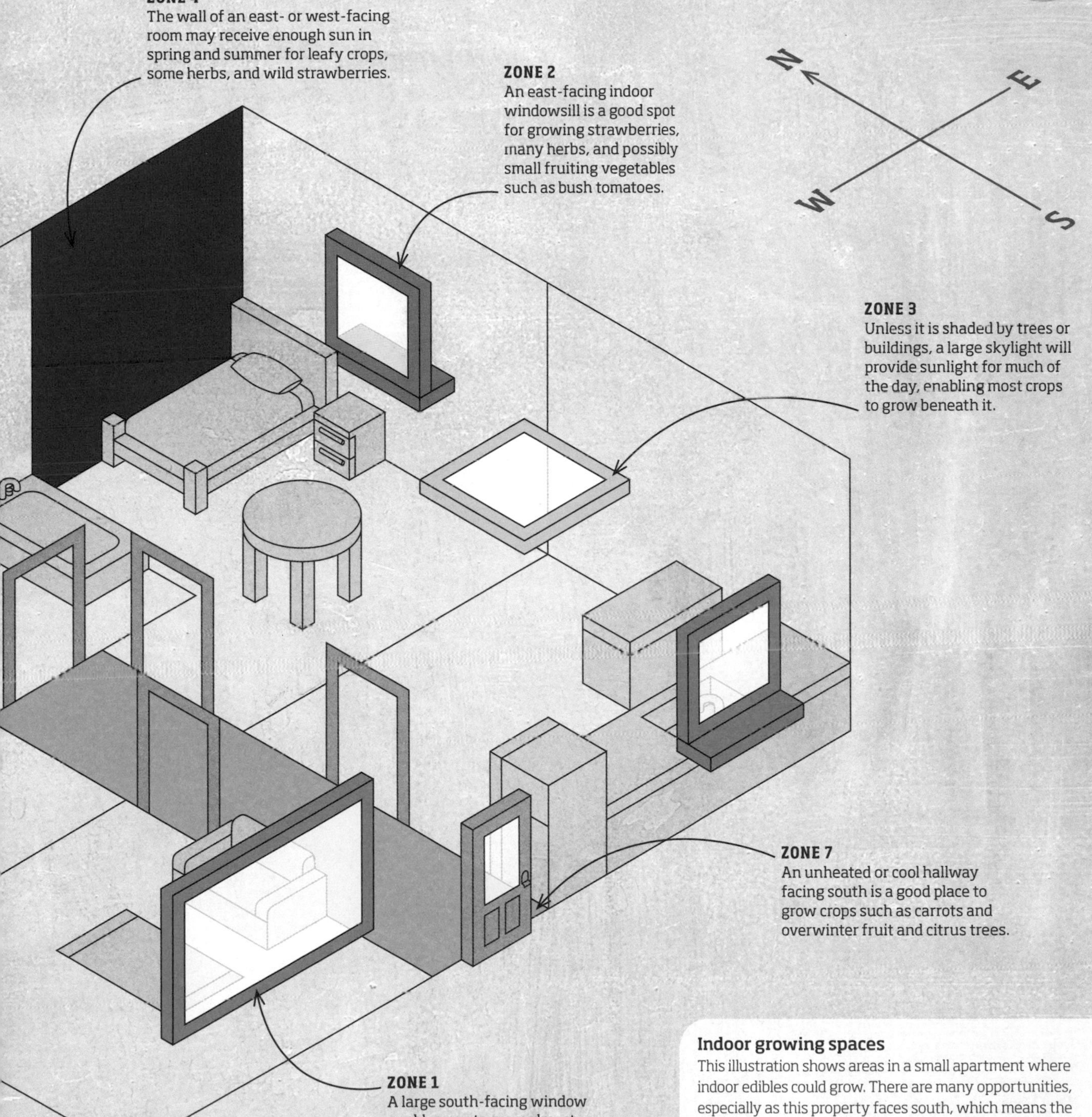

Indoor growing spaces

This illustration shows areas in a small apartment where indoor edibles could grow. There are many opportunities, especially as this property faces south, which means the front room would be bright and sunny for most of the day in spring and summer. Other rooms would provide space for edibles such as leafy crops that require less sunlight.

Bright sunlit zones

Check your home through the day to locate the **brightest, sunniest spots;** rooms that receive direct sun for **six or more hours** a day in summer are best for crops that need good light. These include most **fruit plants** and **herbs**, and **fruiting vegetable crops** such as tomatoes, aubergines, and peppers.

South-facing windows

Most indoor crops that produce fruit, edible flowers, and herbs will thrive by a south-facing window (they may be too hot and bright for lettuces and other salad crops). These areas receive light for most of the day in summer when the plants need sun for healthy leaves or to ripen their fruits.

SUITABLE PLANTS

- **Herbs (most) pp32-75**
- **Edible flowers (summer blooms) pp32-75**
- **Fruiting vegetables pp122-63**
- **Fruits (except wild strawberries) pp164-95**

East- & west-facing windows

While these zones won't receive sun all day, they offer many hours of bright light in spring and summer during the peak growing period. This may be sufficient for fruits to ripen, so try growing the crops listed below. To maximize their exposure to the sun, keep your curtains or blinds open.

SUITABLE PLANTS

- **Herbs (most) pp32-75**
- **Edible flowers pp32-75**
- **Sprouts, leaves & roots pp76-121**
- **Fruiting vegetables pp122-63**
- **Fruits pp164-95**

Zone 3

Beneath a skylight

Skylights are a real boon, as the even top light promotes good growth throughout the day. A skylight and a window will make the room very bright and provide ideal conditions for sun-loving crops such as fruits and fruiting vegetables, but if the room is too hot, leafy vegetables will suffer.

SUITABLE PLANTS

- **Herbs pp32-75**
- **Edible flowers pp32-75**
- **Sprouts, leaves & roots (if the room is not too hot) pp76-121**
- **Fruiting vegetables pp122-63**
- **Fruits (except wild strawberries) pp164-95**

Mediterranean mix pp132-33

Oranges in pots pp180-81

Cucamelons in crates pp156-57

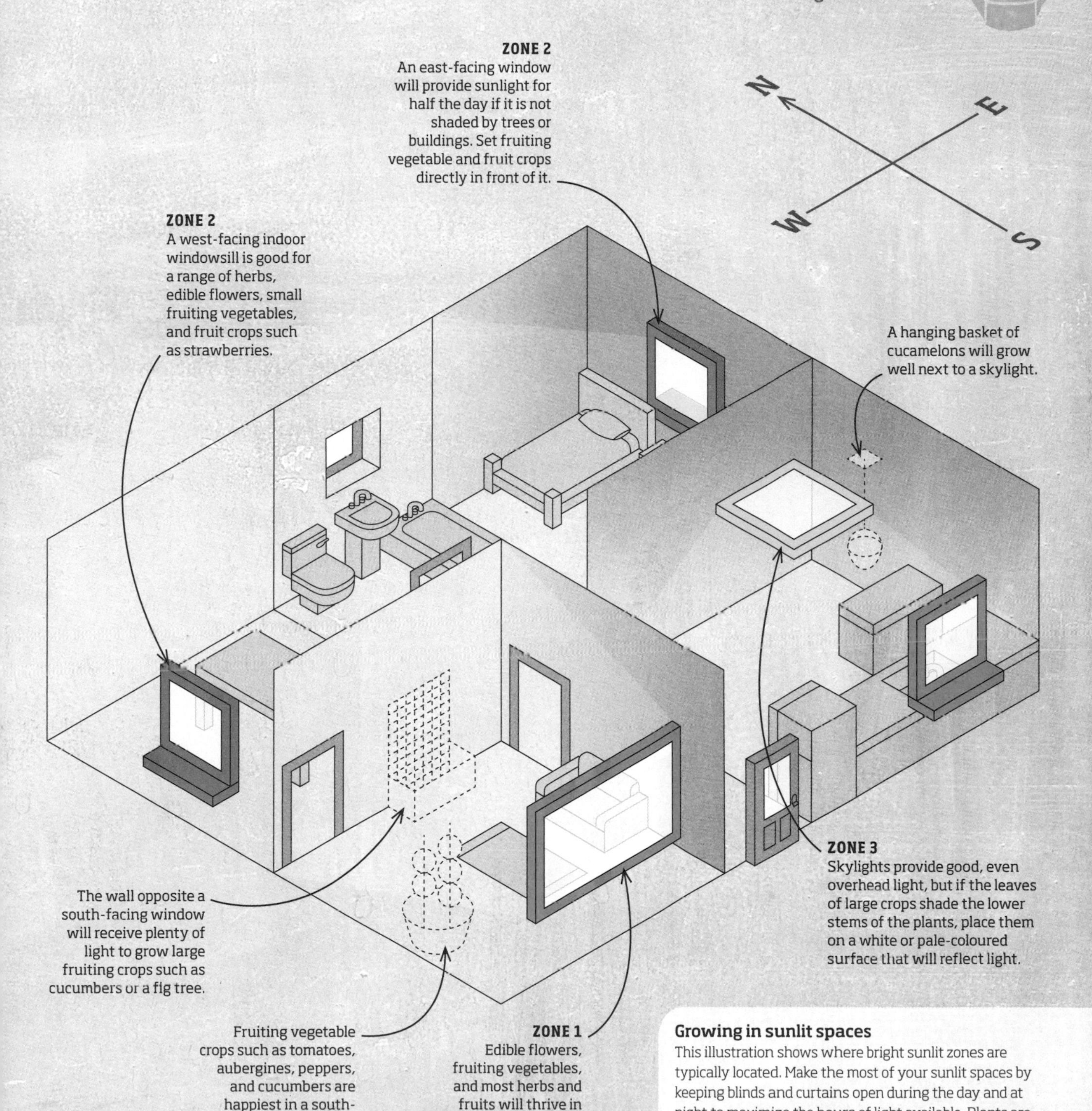

Growing in sunlit spaces

This illustration shows where bright sunlit zones are typically located. Make the most of your sunlit spaces by keeping blinds and curtains open during the day and at night to maximize the hours of light available. Plants are very sensitive to their environment and any extra sun can make the difference between a good or a poor crop.

Partially sunlit zones

Areas that receive **sun** for **part of the day** or even **dark corners** that barely see any light can still be productive spaces for indoor edibles. You can use **mirrors** to illuminate gloomy areas and introduce **grow lights** that imitate the sun, or simply **choose crops**, such as salad leaves, that thrive in **partial shade**.

Zone 4 Walls

The crops you choose for a wall unit or shelf depends on which direction your wall faces and how close it is to natural light. A south-facing wall is classed as zone 1, but a wall facing east or west that receives just a few hours of sunlight a day and a north-facing wall offer less scope for crops.

SUITABLE PLANTS

- Shade-tolerant herbs (eg, mint p66, parsley p72)
- Sprouts pp80-83
- Salad leaves pp96-97
- Small root crops, such as radishes pp110-11
- Wild strawberries pp168-71

Zone 5 Dark corners

Only mushrooms will grow successfully in gloomy areas that receive little or no direct sunlight, but if you introduce a grow light or two your choices will be much greater. Most grow lights are suitable for small plants, so choose compact crops such as herbs, salad leaves, and bush tomatoes.

SUITABLE PLANTS

- Herbs & edible flowers pp32-75
- Microgreens pp88-89
- Mushrooms (no need for grow lights) pp118-21
- Salad leaves pp96-97
- Bush tomatoes pp138-41
- Chilli peppers pp130-31
- Sweet peppers pp162-63

Zone 6 Centre of a room

Salad leaves, sprouts, and root crops will cope well in the centre of a room with a large window that faces east or west and receives some sunlight during the day. (The centre of a small south-facing room falls into zone 1, and the middle of a north-facing room is too dark for most crops.)

SUITABLE PLANTS

- Shade-tolerant herbs (eg, mint p66, parsley p72)
- Edible spring flowers pp56-57
- Edible orchids pp52-55
- Sprouts, leaves & some roots pp76-117
- Wild strawberries pp168-71

Wild strawberries pp168-71

Salad leaves pp90-95

Oriental salad leaves pp98-101

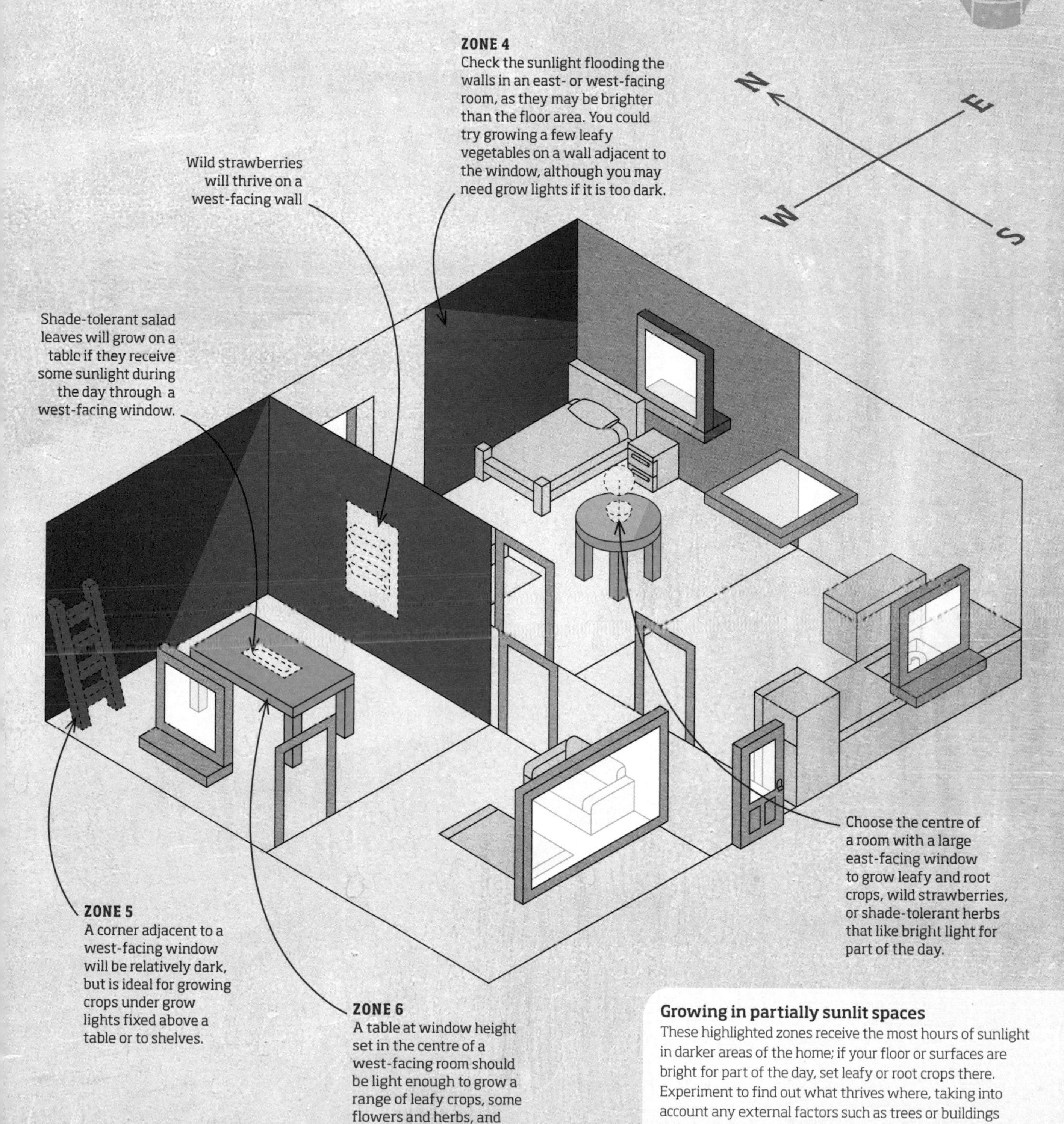

Growing in partially sunlit spaces

These highlighted zones receive the most hours of sunlight in darker areas of the home; if your floor or surfaces are bright for part of the day, set leafy or root crops there. Experiment to find out what thrives where, taking into account any external factors such as trees or buildings that may cast shade and affect the plants' health.

Cool zones

Some plants that are normally **pollinated** by insects are easier to grow on an **outside windowsill** where bees can still reach them, while other crops that hail from Mediterranean climes or areas with a cool winter need **lower temperatures** at this time of year to produce their **fruits** the **following summer**.

Zone 7 Cool (unheated) south-facing room

Grow plants such as strawberries, some herbs, and leafy and root vegetables in this zone all year round. Most fruit trees, including figs, citrus, peaches, and nectarines, need lower temperatures in winter to produce fruits the next year; move them out of a warm, heated room into cooler conditions at this time of year to guarantee their success.

SUITABLE PLANTS

- **Herbs (most) pp32-75**
- **Leafy crops pp76-105**
- **Root vegetables pp106-17**
- **Fruits (over winter) pp164-95**

Outside windowsill

Some outdoor space, such as a windowsill, is useful for a gardener: plants normally pollinated by insects tend to be more productive here. The increase in air circulation also guards against some plant fungal diseases. Tender crops such as tomatoes, peppers, and cucamelons, should not be put outside until all risk of frost has passed in late spring.

SUITABLE PLANTS

- **Herbs & edible flowers (most) pp32-75**
- **Leafy crops pp76-105**
- **Bush tomatoes pp142-43**
- **Chillies pp130-31**
- **Sweet peppers pp162-63**
- **Cucamelons pp156-59**
- **Strawberries pp172-73**

Carrots pp112-15

Geraniums & herbs pp42-45

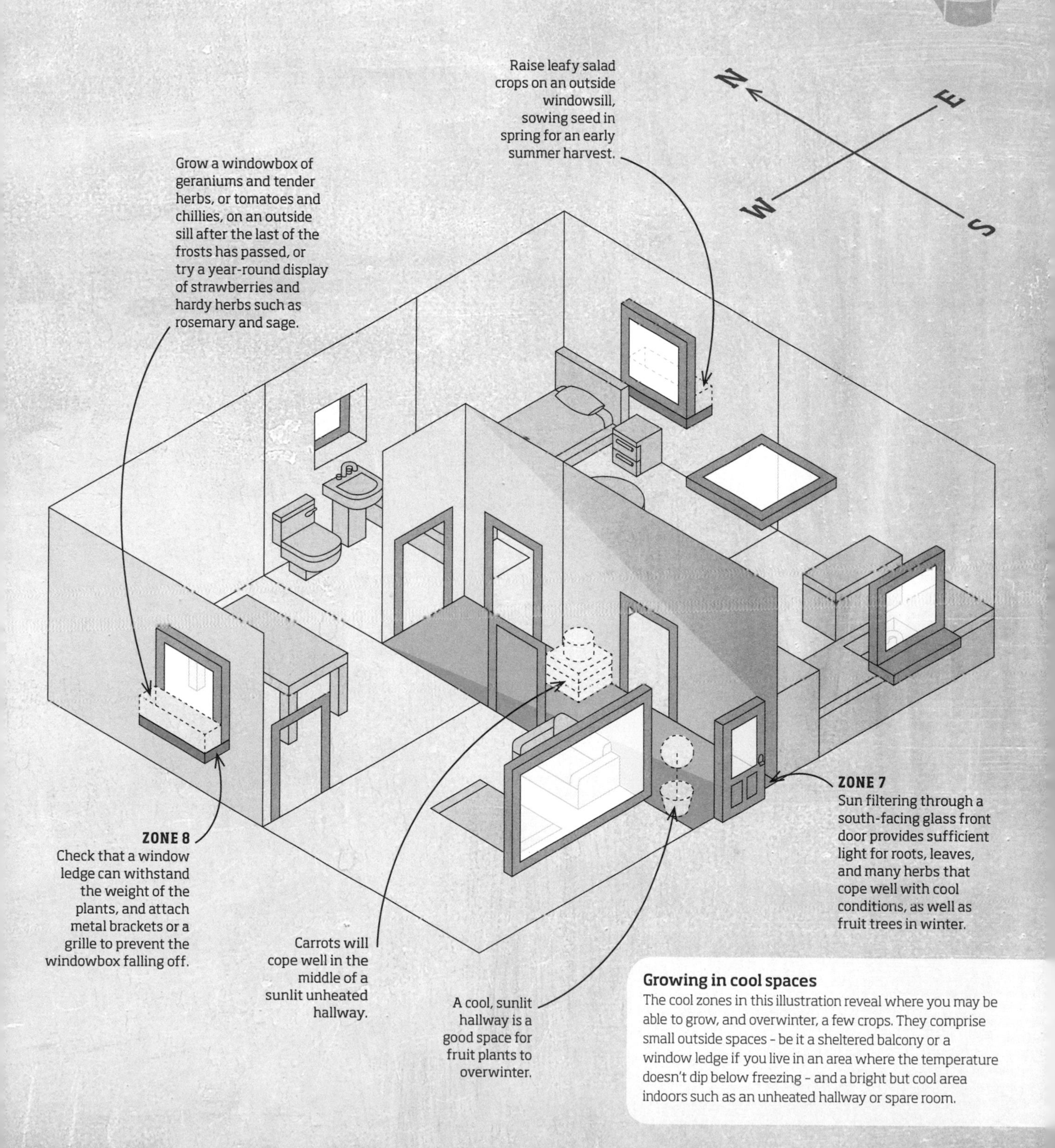

Growing in cool spaces

The cool zones in this illustration reveal where you may be able to grow, and overwinter, a few crops. They comprise small outside spaces - be it a sheltered balcony or a window ledge if you live in an area where the temperature doesn't dip below freezing - and a bright but cool area indoors such as an unheated hallway or spare room.

Best indoor edibles

The edible crops listed here are all **ideal** for **growing in containers** indoors and most are **easy to look after**, providing you with the freshest, tastiest harvests. Refer to individual projects and plant profiles to find out how to grow them.

Herbs & edible flowers

Among the easiest of indoor edibles, most herbs and edible flowers require just a sunny windowsill and warmth to succeed, though mint, tulips, and orchids are happier in bright conditions out of direct sunlight. For more details see pp32–75.

Basil
Annual herb, providing fresh, spicy leaves for many months from spring to autumn.
Zones: 1,2,3

Chives
Mild, onion-flavoured leaves from mid-spring to autumn. Leaves appear year after year but die down each winter and sprout again in spring.
Zones: 1,2,3,7,8

Lemongrass
Grow this tall grass-like plant in a large container in a sunny room or deep windowsill and harvest the lemon-flavoured stems – ideal for Asian dishes – from late spring to late summer.
Zones: 1,2,3

Mint
Tall deciduous herb that produces masses of fresh-flavoured leaves on sturdy stems from late spring to autumn; dies down over winter.
Zones: 2,3,6,7,8

Oregano
A compact deciduous herb with green, yellow or variegated foliage. Leaves appear from spring to autumn but die down each winter.
Zones: 1,2,3,7,8

Parsley
Flat- or curly-leaved varieties both do well in pots in a sunny room, providing leaves from spring to late autumn.
Zones: 1,2,3,7,8

Rosemary
An aromatic shrubby herb, the small needle-like foliage is evergreen, but best only harvested from early spring to late autumn.
Zones: 1,2,3,7,8

Sage
An evergreen shrubby herb that produces fresh green, purple, or variegated new leaves from spring to autumn each year.
Zones: 1,2,3,7,8

Thyme
This small-leaved evergreen herb forms a mound of edible foliage all year; harvest from early spring to late autumn and allow the plant to rest in midwinter when it is not growing.
Zones: 1,2,3,7,8

Dendrobium orchid
The cucumber- and kale-flavoured blooms make beautiful cake decorations.
Zones: 2,3,6,7

Pot marigold
These colourful orange or yellow flowers have a peppery flavour and will bloom all summer if you set them in a sunny area.
Zones: 1,2,3,7,8

Scented pelargonium
Easy to grow on a sunny windowsill. You can eat both the flowers and the foliage.
Zones: 1,2,3,7,8

Tulip
Buy young plants about to flower in spring (dry bulbs planted in autumn won't develop indoors).
Zones: 2,6,7,8

Viola
These diminutive flowers are available in bloom year-round and are easy to grow in small pots.
Zones: 1,2,3,4,7,8

Growing zones
For details of growing zones, see pp16–23.

Zone 1	Zone 2	Zone 3	Zone 4	Zone 5	Zone 6	Zone 7	Zone 8
SOUTH-FACING WINDOWS	OTHER WINDOWS	BENEATH A SKYLIGHT	WALLS	DARK CORNERS	CENTRE OF A ROOM	COOL SOUTH-FACING ROOM	OUTSIDE WINDOWSILL

Sprouts, roots & leaves

It is possible to grow fresh shoots, and a selection of delicious root and leafy crops, in your home. Most leaves do not need bright sunlight (unlike the majority of fruit and vegetables). For more details see pp76–121.

Beetroot
Sow beetroot in spring for a crop of sweet roots later in the summer and autumn.
Zones: 2,6,7,8

Carrots
Long or short varieties are available to grow in pots indoors; sow seeds in spring and summer for two crops later in the year.
Zones: 2,6,7,8

Garlic greens
The bulbs will not bulk up indoors, but you can still enjoy the garlic-flavoured leaves they produce in just a few weeks.
Zones: 1,2,3,7

Lettuce
Green- or red-leaved lettuces can be grown for most of the year in a bright area out of direct sunlight or under a grow light, providing you with fresh salad leaves in an array of colours.
Zones: 2,4,5,6,7,8

Microgreens
One of the easiest crops to grow indoors, microgreens produce fresh, tiny leaves and can be grown year round. There is also a wide selection of flavours and colours to choose from.
Zones: 1,2,3,4,5,7

Mizuna & mibuna
These leafy crops hail from Asia and have a spicy flavour that tastes great in salads and stir-fries. They are easy to grow from seed each year and require similar conditions to salad leaves.
Zones: 2,4,5,6,7,8

Mushroom
You can try a variety of mushrooms, which are easy to grow from kits, all year round, and many are ready to harvest after just a couple of weeks.
Zones: 2,4,5,6,7

Pak choi
These leaves, with their mild mustardy flavour, can be grown as microgreens or larger crops indoors for a summer to autumn harvest.
Zones: 2,4,5,6,7,8

Radish
A fast-maturing crop, the seeds can be sown in pots every month for crunchy radishes in summer and early autumn. The larger white winter radishes should be sown in autumn.
Zones: 2,3,5,6,7,8

Spring onion
The mild-flavoured stems do not take up much space indoors, but they need bright but cool conditions to mature.
Zones: 1,2,3,5,7

Sprouts
Ideal for any home, nutrient-rich sprouts can be grown in glass jars in a bright location such as on a windowsill or kitchen counter.
Zones: 2,3,4

Continued >>

Fruiting vegetables

Colourful fruiting vegetables will add a rich diversity of produce to your home micro-allotment. Chillies, sweet peppers, and patio – also known as bush – tomatoes are ideal for a windowsill, but other crops are larger and will need more space to grow. All require bright sunlight and heat to produce their jewel-like fruits. See pp122–163 for more details.

Aubergine
Keep the plants, which can grow up to 1m (3ft) in height, close to a window in bright sunlight if you want to guarantee a good crop of round or Zeppelin-shaped purple or white fruits.
Zones: 1,2,3

Chilli pepper
These compact woody plants will live from year to year, and are covered with colourful fruits from summer to early autumn. The little white flowers that precede the fruits are pretty, too.
Zones: 1,2,3,8

Cucamelon
These trailing plants can be grown in large hanging baskets in a sunny room, and produce small fruits that look like baby watermelons and taste of cucumber with a hint of lime.
Zones: 1,2,3,8

Cucumber
You need a large sunny room to accommodate this climbing plant, but the tasty fruits, which have much more flavour than those you can buy in the shops, make them worth growing.
Zones: 1,2,3

Sweet pepper
Also known as 'bell' peppers, these compact plants produce large green, yellow, red, or purple fruits in late summer or early autumn. Unlike chillies, sweet peppers have a mild flavour.
Zones: 1,2,3

Tamarillo
If you have a big sunny room to accommodate this large-leaved, handsome plant, you will be rewarded with beautiful yellow or red fruits that taste like a blend of tomato and kiwi fruit.
Zones: 1,2,3

Tomato
For summer or early autumn crops, choose compact bush, or patio, types for hanging baskets and windowsills, or cordon tomatoes with red or yellow fruits that grow up a stake.
Zones: 1,2,3,8

Fruit

Tropical and Mediterranean fruit plants can grow successfully indoors if you have the right conditions, such as a cool room in winter but warmth and bright sunlight in summer. See pp164–195 for more details.

Calamondin
When grown in a sunny area, this diminutive orange will produce a bumper crop of small sour fruits, which are ideal for making marmalade, from late winter to late spring. The plants need to be housed in a cool but bright room in winter.
Zones: 1,2,3,7

Cape gooseberry
These sun-loving bushy plants produce small white flowers, followed in late summer by cherry-sized yellow or orange fruits that are encased in decorative papery husks.
Zones: 1,2,3

Fig
Set a potted plant in a bright room in direct sun, and your fig should produce a few ripe fruits each year from summer to early autumn. The plants need cooler conditions in winter.
Zones: 1,2,3,6,7

Kumquat
Tall and elegant, kumquat plants produce pear-shaped fruits with edible skins from early spring to summer, but to grow successfully the following year they need a cool room in winter.
Zones: 1,2,3,7

Lemon
These beautiful plants need bright sunny conditions for a good crop of fruits to develop and ripen, but also require a cool but bright room in the winter when they are resting.
Zones: 1,2,3,7

Lime
Very similar in size and appearance to lemon trees, limes need a bright, sunny, warm location from spring to early autumn and a cool but bright room in winter. The makrut lime differs slightly in appearance from other limes with its large divided leaves and knobbly green fruits.
Zones: 1,2,3,7

Mandarin
This is a variety of orange plant, and requires heat and bright sun from late spring to autumn when the fruits are starting to develop, followed by cool conditions throughout the winter.
Zones: 1,2,3,7

Nectarine
Nectarines, like their close cousins, peaches, produce sweet juicy fruits in summer, but you will need to fertilize the flowers by hand to ensure they fruit when growing them indoors.
Zones: 1,2,3,7

Orange
As well as the delicious fruits, these citrus trees also produce scented blossoms that will perfume your home. Keep the plants in a bright, sunny spot in summer, and a cool but bright room during the winter.
Zones: 1,2,3,7

Peach
The peach tree's sweet furry-skinned fruits appear in summer, and require bright sunlight to ripen. Keep the tree in cooler conditions in winter after it has lost its leaves.
Zones: 1,2,3,7

Pineapple guava
The fruits of this evergreen tropical plant, which appear in late summer or autumn, are small and sweet with a pineapple flavour. The flowers are also edible. This shrub requires bright sunlight and warmth in summer, but keep it in a cooler room in the winter.
Zones: 1,2,3,7

Strawberry
Choose from wild or alpine strawberries, which produce small fruits over many weeks from late spring, or plants with full-sized strawberries that ripen in summer or early autumn. These regular strawberries need a bright position to produce the best crops, but the wild types will fruit in areas that are out of direct sunlight.
Zones: 1,2,3,4,6,7,8

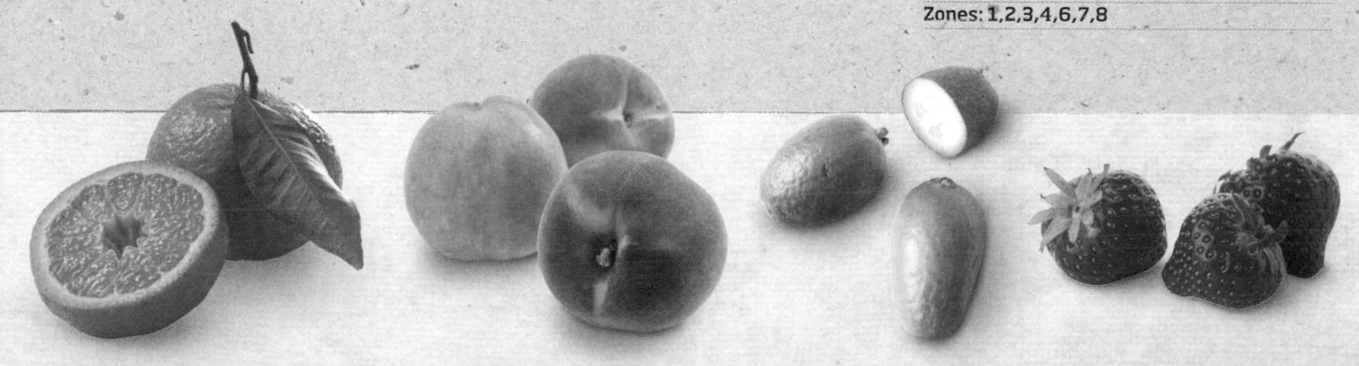

Choosing a container

There are some **important factors** to consider when you choose a **pot or container** for your fruit and vegetables. Before you settle on its style and material (pp30–31), ensure it meets all the **practical aspects** required.

Basic requirements

Before buying a container, first make sure that it will meet the needs of the indoor edibles you are planning to grow. Selecting a pot of the right size (see opposite) is crucial if you want your plants to thrive. And although the outer casings of all your containers must be waterproof so they don't leak dirty water onto your floors or furniture, few edible plants like to sit in soggy soil, so you should also consider how water can drain away easily without creating a mess.

Drainage essentials

The simplest way to combine these two elements is to use a container with drainage holes at the bottom and sit it on a tray or deep saucer, which will capture any excess water (see illustration, top right).

Another option is to plant your edible crops in a plastic pot with drainage holes and place the pot inside a waterproof decorative container, also known as a "sleeve" (see illustration, centre right). Alternatively, if you want to plant your crops directly into a container, fill the base with a layer of gravel at least 2.5cm (1in) deep to create a "well" for the water to drain into and place a plastic liner punctured with drainage holes over the gravel before you add compost.

You can also buy specially-designed containers that incorporate a drainage system and reservoir at the bottom (see illustration, below right). These are often labelled "self-watering" because water in the reservoir feeds back into the compost.

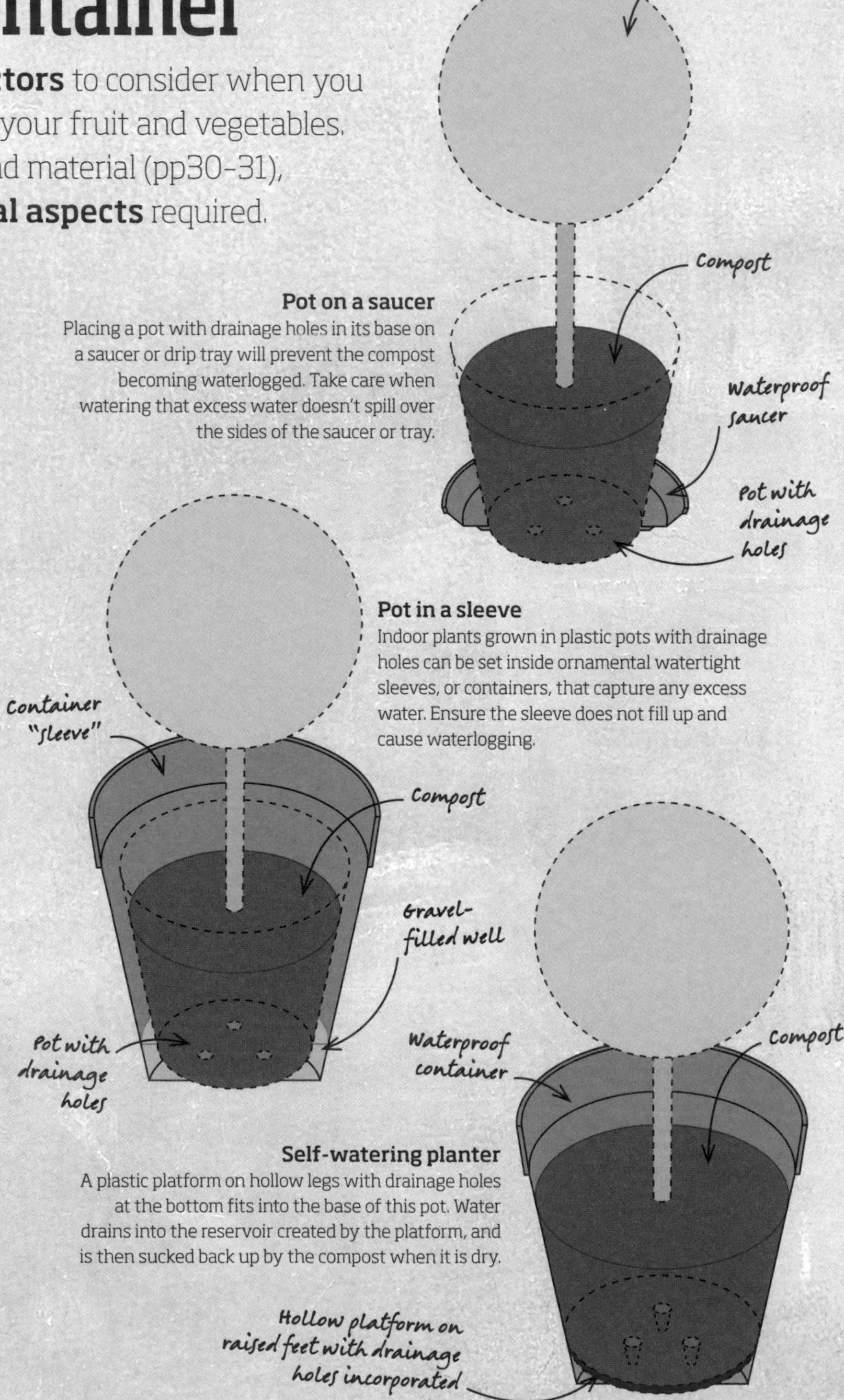

Pot on a saucer
Placing a pot with drainage holes in its base on a saucer or drip tray will prevent the compost becoming waterlogged. Take care when watering that excess water doesn't spill over the sides of the saucer or tray.

Pot in a sleeve
Indoor plants grown in plastic pots with drainage holes can be set inside ornamental watertight sleeves, or containers, that capture any excess water. Ensure the sleeve does not fill up and cause waterlogging.

Self-watering planter
A plastic platform on hollow legs with drainage holes at the bottom fits into the base of this pot. Water drains into the reservoir created by the platform, and is then sucked back up by the compost when it is dry.

Size matters

The size of the plants you intend to grow will determine the size of pot you need. Large plants and trees, such as oranges and lemons, will require plenty of root room, and because many live for a number of years, they will also need to be repotted into larger containers as they grow. To avoid spending money on expensive containers each time you repot, you could plant into plastic pots and slip those inside an oversized decorative container, which will accommodate the growing plant for a few years.

Calculating a plant's needs

Tall plants, such as cordon tomatoes, will need a pot at least 25cm (10in) deep and 20cm (8in) wide to accommodate the roots and provide the tall stems – which need to be tied to canes as they grow upwards – with some stability.

Small edibles such as radishes do not need much space individually, but for a reasonable crop it is easier to plant them en masse in a large pot with room for ten or more plants. Plants from dry climates, such as herbs and figs, will grow in more cramped conditions, as they do not require lots of compost and water to thrive.

Crops in pots that offer no space for drainage are more susceptible to fungal diseases

Leave a good gap between the top of the compost and the rim of the pot so water won't spill out.

Thyme will be happy in a small container.

Small containers

While tiny pots look great, not many edible plants will survive for long in them. Choose small herb plants, flowers and microgreens for these containers, but remember that they will need watering more frequently than larger types.

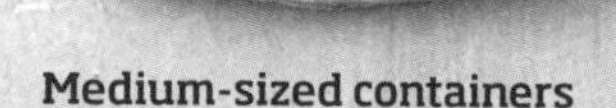

Medium-sized containers

Many crops, including tomatoes, peppers, chillies and herbs, will thrive in containers measuring 25–38cm (10–15in) in diameter and the same in depth. Also use them for multiples of smaller crops, such as salad leaves and carrots.

Large containers

Big containers hold more compost and water than smaller ones, which means you will not need to water them as frequently. They also provide stability for large trees although some, such as figs, perform best when their roots are restricted.

Types of container

The material from which a container or pot is made not only affects the way it looks but also its longevity and weight. **Light pots** are a **good choice**, as they are easy to move around indoors, while containers made from **heavy materials** help to **anchor** larger plants and fruit trees. Take a look at the containers showcased here to help you choose the right pots for your home.

Terracotta and glazed clay pots can be heavy once planted up.

Line artisan-style crates and baskets before planting.

Glazed clay & terracotta

Terracotta and glazed clay pots lend a rustic, earthy look to indoor displays, but are porous and should not be set directly onto carpets, wooden floors, or other delicate flooring. Stand both types of pot on waterproof trays to prevent staining.

Wood & basketry

Natural planters suit modern and traditional decors. As they aren't waterproof, line them with plastic to prevent them rotting or their contents staining furniture and flooring. Plant crops in plastic pots with drainage holes first and put them inside the lined containers.

Hanging containers

Most hanging baskets are not waterproof, but they can be lined with plastic or a washing-up or mixing bowl to create the right conditions for growing crops indoors.

Fill the base of sealed containers with polystyrene pieces to create an area for water to drain into.

Small herb plants will thrive in a hanging pot.

Choose a material that suits your style and shows off your plants to their best effect

Metal heats up quickly, so plants will need watering frequently.

Fibreglass and resin pots are lightweight and versatile.

Plastic pots often incorporate a tray or hidden water reservoir.

Metal & faux metals

True and faux metals enhance a contemporary industrial design, or you can choose a classic fake lead pot for a more traditional interior. Most are also light and easy to move around, but not all are waterproof, so line with plastic before planting if necessary.

Fibreglass, resin & plastics

Containers made from fibreglass and resin come in traditional and contemporary styles, and are a good choice for indoor planting. Plain plastic pots with drainage holes in the base can be inserted in waterproof containers to create a decorative display.

Herbs & edible flowers

Discover the wide range of herbs - among the easiest crops to grow indoors - that thrive in pots, and plants that produce flowers you can eat. Try a few of the projects that enable you to grow these colourful edibles in your home.

Introducing herbs & edible flowers

Just a few pots of **fresh herbs** and **edible flowers** growing in your home will provide the **essential ingredients** for an array of dishes and drinks.

What is a herb?

While herbs grow just like any other plant, what sets them apart is the intense flavour of their edible leaves and their traditional health-giving properties. The varieties included in this book, such as thyme, mint, and basil, are universally valued by cooks for their unique taste and aroma in sweet and savoury recipes. Many fresh herbs contain essential minerals and vitamins, such as A and C, and can benefit your health in other ways, too. For example, mint leaves taken as a tisane, or hot tea, can aid digestion, while research has shown that the smell of rosemary and sage can help improve cognitive skills and memory retention. Herbs are rewarding plants to grow indoors since most can be raised in containers by a sunny window, offering an abundance of fresh leaves close to hand as you cook.

The power of flowers

Many edible flowers are surprisingly tasty and can be used to both flavour and decorate fresh salads, desserts, cakes, and even bread. They can also add a few vitamins to your cuisine; some, such as lavender, are sources of antioxidants, which promote good health and keep diseases at bay.

It's worth growing a few different varieties through the year: the exquisite blooms will inject colour into your indoor edible schemes, lifting your spirits, and you can change the display every few months to reflect the seasons, starting in spring with tulips and bellis daisies, then moving on to summer flowers. The plants will keep on giving, too, as in many cases the more blooms you pick the more they produce; plants such as pot marigolds, violas, primroses, and geraniums will perform over a long period, although tulips will bloom just once before fading.

Best zones for herbs & flowers

All flowers and herbs will perform best in bright light conditions, and grow well in zones 1, 2 or 3. Certain plants will also grow in partially sunlit zones, but you will need to install grow lights for any darker areas in your home.

South-facing windows
All herbs and edible flowers will do well here, but keep them well watered as these sills become very hot in summer and on sunny spring and autumn days.

East- and west-facing windows
All herbs and edible flowers will be happy set directly in front of an east- or west-facing window, although basil and lavender may not do as well here as in zone 1.

Beneath a skylight
All herbs and edible flowers perform well under a skylight, especially if there is supplementary light from a vertical window. Water plants regularly in rooms that get hot.

Walls
Sunny walls will suit all herbs and edible flowers. However, opt for mint, oregano, parsley, orchids, and violas for any walls that are shaded for part of the day.

Dark corners
All herbs and edible flowers can be grown in dark corners if you set them under a grow light. However, without this supplementary lighting most would fail.

Centre of a room
All herbs and edible flowers will be happy in the middle of a bright, sunlit room. Grow orchids, oregano, parsley, violas, or mint if it is out of direct sun for part of the day.

Cool (unheated) south-facing room
All herbs and edible flowers will grow in cool bright conditions, except basil, which needs a little more heat but may thrive here during the summer months.

Outside windowsill
All herbs and edible flowers except orchids will grow well here. Basil needs to be protected from frost, so do not plant this out until temperatures rise in late spring.

Herbs & edible flowers in pots for a windowsill

Fragrant herbs and edible flowers arranged in pretty pots on a **kitchen windowsill** make a beautiful feature and provide an array of **fresh culinary leaves and blooms** to use (see project overleaf).

MINT
One of the few herbs that prefers cooler conditions, mint will grow alongside sun-loving plants if you keep the compost damp at all times, but guard against waterlogging.

VIOLAS
Perfect for adding colour to salads or cakes, violas inject lively visual interest to a container display. These undemanding plants will flower for many weeks and thrive in small pots if watered regularly.

PARSLEY
There are a few parsley varieties to choose from (see pp72–73) and all grow well in containers. Although these herbs live for two years, the leaves are most tender and flavoursome in their first year.

ROSEMARY
In spring, this woody-stemmed versatile herb is covered in tiny blue flowers, which are also edible. Given the chance, rosemary will grow into quite a large shrub, and will only be happy in a pot for a few seasons.

Potting up herbs & flowers

Most herbs and edible flowers will be happy on a bright windowsill and you can harvest the leaves and blooms for most of the year, although pick them sparingly in winter when the plants do not grow very much. Choose a selection for a variety of flavours and uses.

Choosing culinary herbs

Among the easiest to grow and most versatile herbs in the kitchen use are those outlined below. If you do not have much windowsill space, opt for just a few of your favourites so you will always have sufficient leaves to hand. Never strip a plant of all or most of its foliage, as this will kill it.

Turn your herb and flower pots around every day or two so that each part of the plant grows equally as it seeks the light and doesn't become leggy on one side

Chives

Sage

Violas

Thyme

SAGE
This Mediterranean herb thrives in a pot for a year or two, but will then need replacing or potting up into a larger container. Place your sage on a sunny windowsill and ensure the soil does not become waterlogged.

THYME
Choose from a range of thymes (see pp40–41), which are easy to grow. Some reach 30cm (12in) in height and will need a larger pot than the container shown here. Keep moist, but guard against soggy compost.

CHIVES
This grass-like, onion-flavoured herb grows well in a pot on a windowsill, but does require full sun. Harvest from spring to autumn; the plants die down over winter, but shoots will emerge again the following spring.

Quick growing guide

30 minutes to pot up

Full sunlight 10-22°C (50-72°F)

Water only when top of compost feels dry

Feed every 2-4 weeks from late spring to autumn with a fertilizer for leafy crops

Snip leaves as needed when plants are in full growth

Project >>

Grow herbs & flowers in pots

Although herbs and flowers are among the **easiest edibles** to grow indoors, they require plenty of **drainage**, and are best grown in **plastic pots** with holes in the base, which can be easily inserted inside decorative containers.

YOU WILL NEED

- herbs - choose a variety (see pp40-41, 46-47, 66-67, 72-75)
- edible flowers, such as violas (see pp56-57 for other ideas)
- plastic pots to fit inside decorative containers of your choice
- soil-based potting compost, such as John Innes no 1
- horticultural sand
- gravel
- decorative pots
- small watering can

1 You can buy many herbs in plastic pots and just slip them into decorative containers with a layer of gravel in the base to prevent waterlogging. However, rosemary and sage in particular will soon outgrow small containers and need potting on. To do this, line the base of a plastic pot with soil-based compost. Mix a little horticultural sand in with the compost to make it more free-draining.

2 Water the plant, then tip it out of its original container, placing your fingers between the stems to avoid damaging them. Set the plant on the compost and check the rootball is sitting just below the rim of the new pot.

Transplant your rosemary into a pot a couple of sizes larger than its original one.

Turn your herb plants in their pots upside down to check the root system, and repot any that have long roots growing out of the drainage holes

3 Gently fill in around the herb with more compost; do not bury the stems or they may rot. Firm the compost gently with your fingers, then water the plant well.

Check that you leave no air gaps when filling in around the plant

You can use gravel or small pieces of polystyrene in the base of the outer pot.

4 Add a layer of gravel to the bottom of your decorative pot. This will raise the herb slightly off the bottom, allowing excess water to drain into this area. Put the repotted herb into its final container.

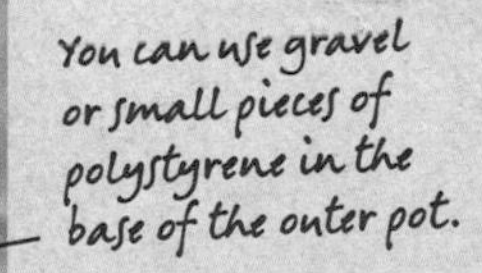

Aftercare

Few herbs or flowers will be happy in containers measuring less than 9cm (3½in) in diameter and 12cm (5in) deep, although some, including thyme and violas, will cope in tiny pots for a short while – but do not take any leaves from small herbs. Any plants in small pots will need repotting after a couple of months. Only water your herbs and flowers when the top of the compost feels dry, and don't add too much. If the top of the compost is glistening with water, tip away the excess. Water the plant again only when the compost feels dry. Feed every two to four weeks from late spring to autumn with a liquid fertilizer designed for leafy crops.

Potted herbs with a thin layer of gravel on top to help the compost stay moist.

Thyme

Thymus species

A decorative addition to an indoor garden, thyme thrives on a sunny windowsill and can be harvested from spring to autumn. Add the leaves to soups, sauces, fish, and meat dishes.

Common thyme produces small pink flowers in summer, which can be eaten together with the leaves.

How to grow

When to buy or sow

Young plants are available all year; if you buy in winter, don't harvest the leaves until spring, when new growth appears. Repot plants with congested roots into slightly larger containers filled with soil-based compost, such as John Innes no 1, mixed with horticultural sand or grit.

Light & heat

Thyme is hardy, but needs a sunny location to succeed; it likes warmth in summer, but keep it cooler in winter. Increase the ventilation by opening the windows. It will also be happy on a sunny outside windowsill or balcony year-round.

Watering

Like all Mediterranean herbs, thyme thrives in free-draining compost and may rot in waterlogged soil. Plant it in a pot with drainage holes in the bottom to maintain the correct moisture level, and water only when the top of the compost feels dry.

Aftercare

Feed every two weeks from spring to early autumn with an all-purpose liquid fertilizer for leafy crops. Repot every year or two in spring in a 3:1 mix of soil-based compost and horticultural grit.

Harvesting

Harvest a few leaves from each plant at any one time from early spring to late autumn. Although thyme is an evergreen shrub, leave the plant to rest in winter.

Common thyme

Best indoor varieties

Buy a selection of thymes to provide a wealth of colourful foliage on a windowsill, as well as leaves for cooking. Some forms, such as lemon thymes, have distinctive aromas, while low-lying creeping types look pretty trailing from wide, shallow containers.

COMMON THYME ▶
(*Thymus vulgaris*)
This plain green variety is easy to grow and the traditional flavour of its leaves is ideal for meat and fish dishes.
Height & spread: 30 x 30cm (12 x 12in)

ALPINE THYME ▶
(*Thymus* 'Worfield Gardens')
This compact thyme has white variegated leaves with red new growth which makes a beautiful display. The leaves have a refreshing, zesty flavour.
Height & spread: 10 x 20cm (4 x 8in)

WILD THYME ▶
(*Thymus serpyllum*)
Grow this thyme, with its highly scented spiky leaves and pink flowers, in a wide, shallow pot, and use the leaves in stews and casseroles.
Height & spread: 10 x 30cm (4 x 12in)

LEMON THYME ▲
(*Thymus pulegioides* 'Archer's Gold')
The aromatic lemon-scented leaves of this thyme are perfect for chicken and fish recipes.
Height & spread: 25 x 25cm (10 x 10in)

'SILVER POSIE' ▶
(*Thymus* 'Silver Posie')
A bushy, creeping thyme, with white-edged grey-green leaves and purple to white flowers in late spring and early summer. Use in bouquets garnis, stuffings, and sauces.
Height & spread: 30 x 30cm (12 x 12in)

CREEPING RED THYME ▶
(*Thymus* 'Coccineus Group')
This mat-forming thyme is ideal for the edge of a big pot with a tall herb, such as sage, in the centre. It produces pink flowers in early summer. Use in meat and fish dishes.
Height & spread: 10 x 20cm (4 x 8in)

Boosting flavour

Scatter thyme leaves over roast meats and fish to boost their flavour.
Add to bouquets garnis with parsley and bay leaves for casseroles and stews.
Sprinkle a little over feta and honey for a Greek-inspired pancake topping.
Mix lemon thyme leaves with olive oil, lemon juice, mustard, seasoning, and a little sugar to make a zesty vinaigrette for vegetables.
Crush thyme leaves with sea salt flakes and sprinkle over potatoes or leafy greens.
Thyme with chicken or turkey make great partners; sprinkle some roughly chopped fresh leaves on top of the bird just before roasting it, or add the leaves to the stuffing mix.

Roast chicken with thyme

Choose a sunny windowsill for your herbs and flowers. They will cope with shade for a few hours each day, but will fail to thrive if positioned on a gloomy north-facing windowsill.

Scented geranium & herb windowbox

Utilize **any outdoor space**, such as a windowsill, to extend your range of edible crops. A **mix of herbs and geranium flowers** provides you with fresh ingredients as well as a beautiful, **long-lasting** display (see project overleaf).

Using your outdoor space

An exterior windowsill provides a good growing environment for many compact crops, offering bright light, relative warmth, and shelter. You can plant up the windowbox indoors before positioning it on your windowsill, and then tend the plants from inside. Ensure the box is fixed securely to the sill, and water the plants as frequently as you would if they were indoors, even during rainy weather, since most sills are protected from the elements. Flowering herbs such as thyme and basil will help to feed the bee population, too.

Pest-free crops
A strip of copper tape fixed to the outside of the windowbox will help deter any slugs and snails.

Choosing geraniums & herbs

Most herbs and edible flowers will thrive in a windowbox, but choose the largest possible container that will fit your windowsill to give the plants plenty of space to develop.

Scented geranium
This drought-tolerant plant is easy to grow. Infuse cordials with its crushed leaves to add subtle flavour, and use the flowers as a garnish.

Creeping thyme
Choose this trailing variety to soften the edges of the display. Use its leaves in the same way as common thyme.

Sorrel
Red-veined sorrel is the prettiest variety of this herb. Use in soups, salads, and fish dishes to inject a spicy, bitter taste.

Quick growing guide

2 hours

Full sun or light shade

Water every day or two

Feed with all-purpose liquid fertilizer (see overleaf)

Pick flowers and leaves as needed

Project >>

Plant a geranium & herb windowbox

This **easy planting project** is ideal for those new to gardening, and will provide you with a continuous supply of **flowers and leaves** that can be harvested through the **summer** and **early autumn**.

If you don't have an outside sill, fix some metal brackets securely to a wall below a window

YOU WILL NEED

- windowbox, measuring approx 45 x 20 x 20cm (18 x 8 x 8in)
- polystyrene pieces
- multi-purpose compost
- 2 x scented geraniums (pelargonium varieties such as 'Orange Fizz' and 'Attar of Roses')
- 1 x red-veined sorrel (*Rumex sanguineus*)
- 1 x creeping thyme (*Thymus serpyllum*)
- 1 x variegated oregano (*Oreganum vulgare* 'Country Cream')
- 1 x Thai basil (*Ocimum basilicum* var. *thyrsiflorum*)
- watering can
- all-purpose liquid fertilizer

The geranium leaves will infuse your home with scent when the windows are open

1 If your windowbox does not have drainage holes, drill a few in the bottom. Add a thin layer of polystyrene pieces to the base of the box – these will help to prevent the drainage holes becoming blocked – followed by a layer of multi-purpose compost.

Use multi-purpose compost enriched with fertilizer.

2 Set the largest geranium – the variety 'Orange Fizz' is shown here – on the compost and check the top of the rootball sits at least 2.5cm (1in) below the rim.

3 If the plant's roots are tightly bound around the rootball, gently tease them out with your fingers, as shown. This will allow them to expand more easily.

4 Plant up the other herbs and flowers, with the basil and sorrel at the back and a spreading geranium to one side. Ensure all are set 2.5cm (1in) below the rim of the box.

5 Finally, tuck in a creeping thyme at the front, where it will not be too shaded by the other plants' leaves. Firm the compost around all the rootballs with your fingers.

6 Set the planted windowbox on an outside sill (or indoors on a tray on a sunny sill) and water well. Make sure the windowbox is sitting securely on the sill, and fix a metal bracket underneath if necessary to prevent it falling off.

Pick herb leaves regularly to encourage more to grow.

Aftercare

If you have used a multi-purpose compost enriched with fertilizers, you will not need to feed the plants for a few weeks. You can then add an all-purpose liquid feed if the plants start to look lacklustre. Remove any dead and fading flowers to encourage the plants to produce more blooms.

Removing faded geranium blooms

Basil

Ocimum species

An indispensable aromatic herb, basil is the perfect accompaniment for fresh tomatoes and Mediterranean-inspired dishes. There are many varieties, offering a range of leaf colours and flavours.

Spice basil

How to grow

When to buy or sow

Sow basil seed in spring in pots of good-quality seed compost, or buy young plants from a garden centre in late spring, when they are readily available. If you buy mature basil, plant it in multi-purpose compost.

Light & heat

Sun-loving basil needs lots of light, and is best grown on a south-facing windowsill. It will be happy in a warm room, but keep the windows open to increase ventilation during hot summer weather.

Watering

Basil is quite fussy when it comes to watering. The plants like damp but free-draining conditions; in wet or waterlogged compost they quickly succumb to fungal diseases. Ensure the pot in which the basil is planted has plenty of drainage holes and water it every two to three days. Try to avoid wetting the leaves, as this will also protect your basil from disease.

Aftercare

When mature, feed your plants every two weeks with an all-purpose liquid fertilizer for leafy crops. Remove any flower stems before they produce seed.

Harvesting

Pinch off the leafy tips as you need them, taking a few sprigs at a time. Avoid removing lower, woody sections, which will cause the plant to die back.

Best indoor varieties

As well as the common green sweet basil, there are purple-leaved forms and those with fruity or highly spiced flavours. For a citrus note, try lemon or lime basil, which offer traditional flavours combined with refreshing aromas. Garden centres sell a range of young basil plants, but your choice of varieties will be wider if you choose to grow your plants from seed.

SWEET BASIL ▲
(*Ocimum basilicum*)
This is the common basil you will find in supermarkets. Its clove-scented foliage makes it a great partner for tomato dishes and it's ideal for pesto sauces.
Height & spread: 25 x 25cm (10 x 10in)

SPICE BASIL ▶
(*Ocimum basilicum* 'Spice')
Similar to sweet basil, this plant produces spikes of pretty pink flowers that add to its decorative value. It has a sweet, spicy taste and can be used in salads and Mediterranean-style dishes.
Height & spread: 25 x 25cm (10 x 10in)

◀ 'DARK OPAL'
(*Ocimum basilicum* 'Dark Opal')
One of the purple-leaved basils, it has a mild spicy flavour. It requires full sunlight and good drainage to thrive. Water plants sparingly, allowing the top of the compost to dry out between watering.
Height & spread: 30 x 30cm (12 x 12in)

◀ BUSH BASIL
(*Ocimum minimum* 'Bush')
Also known as Greek basil, this dwarf form has small leaves and a strong, spicy taste. It is a little less likely to succumb to mildew than its cousins.
Height & spread: 20 x 20cm (8 x 8in)

THAI BASIL ▶
(*Ocimum basilicum* var. *thyrsiflorum*)
Also called cinnamon basil, it has pretty purple stems and the leaves have a spicy, liquorice taste. It is often used in Asian-style dishes and stir-fries.
Height & spread: 30 x 30cm (12 x 12in)

LEMON BASIL ▶
(*Ocimum* x *citriodorum*)
This light-green leaved form has a citrus flavour and is ideal for fish and Asian dishes, or use it raw in salads to add a tantalizing zing. Also try the similar lime basil. **Height & spread:** 30 x 30cm (12 x 12in)

Ideas to try

One of the best ways to enjoy the fresh leaves is in a classic tricolore salad of basil, tomatoes, and mozzarella cheese.

Blend basil leaves with lemon juice, honey, and cold water to make lemonade.

Purée basil with lime juice and sugar syrup, and freeze for an unusual sorbet.

Blitz Thai basil with baby spinach, coriander, avocado, olive oil, and a pinch of salt and sugar for an Asian-style pesto sauce.

To make Caprese farro salad, add cooked protein-rich farro grains (or brown rice or quinoa if you prefer) to a classic tricolore salad (see below) and top with a simple olive oil dressing.

Tricolore salad

Pick only the leafy stem tips to encourage the plants to produce more shoots

Choose lightweight plastic, wooden, or metal waterproof containers to house your pots of tea herbs, and make sure you distribute the plants evenly along the shelves so they do not tip up.

Grow your own herbal teas

Fresh herbal teas have many health and medicinal benefits. Choose a **range of herbs** and let them flourish on a set of **home-made hanging shelves** in front of a window – ideal if you want to pack lots of plants into a **small space** to enjoy a daily cup of herbal tea (see project overleaf).

Healthy leaf tea

Herbal teas are caffeine-free and high in antioxidants, but many have additional benefits. Mint tea soothes stomach ache and relieves nausea, and can keep you alert, chamomile calms the nerves and aids sleep, and lemon verbena tea is thought to reduce joint pain.

Choosing plants for herbal teas

Herbal plants to grow include chamomile, stevia (*Stevia rebaudiana*; see also p221), feverfew, lemon verbena, and peppermint (see below). Most like full sun, but they grow well near any window except one facing north.

Mint tea promotes good digestion

Feverfew
(*Tanacetum parthenium*)
Grow this member of the daisy family in a large pot of well-drained compost. Its leaves are thought to help relieve migraines and muscular aches and pains.

Lemon verbena
(*Aloysia citrodora*)
Keep this shrubby plant from growing too tall by picking the leafy tips regularly. It will drop its leaves in winter and grow new leaves the following spring.

Peppermint
(*Mentha x piperita*)
Plant a few large pots of this fast-growing herb and keep it going from year to year - it is a deciduous plant, so new growth will appear each spring.

Quick growing guide

2-3 hours for various stages

Full sun or part shade

Water every 2-3 days

After 6 weeks, feed fortnightly with fertilizer for leafy crops

Snip off stem tips as required

Project >>

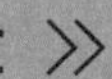

Make suspended shelves for herbs

These stylish wooden shelves take just a short while to make, and will allow you to utilize the **full length of your window** for growing a **range of tea herbs**. You can even adjust the space between the shelves to accommodate taller plants.

YOU WILL NEED

- 2 x pieces of timber, approximately 60 x 20 x 2cm (24 x 8 x 3/4in), cut to size and sanded so the edges are smooth
- pencil
- tape measure
- screwdriver and drill bit
- 8m (26ft) sash cord or rope
- clothes pegs
- herbs, such as mint and lemon verbena, to use for making tea
- multi-purpose compost
- vermiculite (or perlite)
- plastic pots with drainage holes
- decorative lightweight waterproof pots
- watering can

For a more colourful effect, use dyed cord or rope and paint the wooden shelves in a bright shade

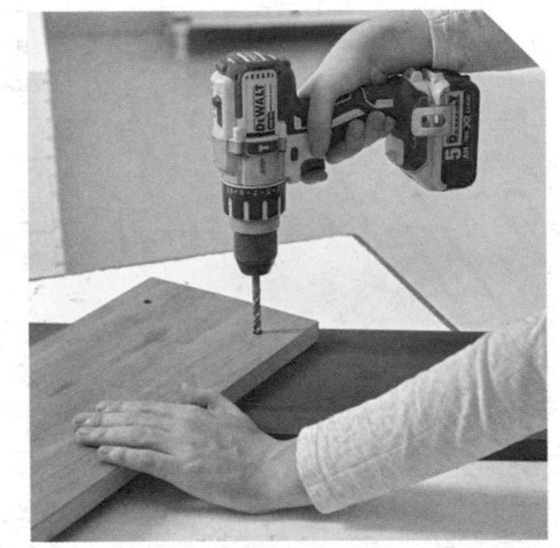

1 Make a pencil mark in each corner of both pieces of wood 2cm (3/4in) from the edge. To drill through the marked points, place each piece of wood on an old table or scrap wood. Make holes large enough for the sash cord to fit through easily.

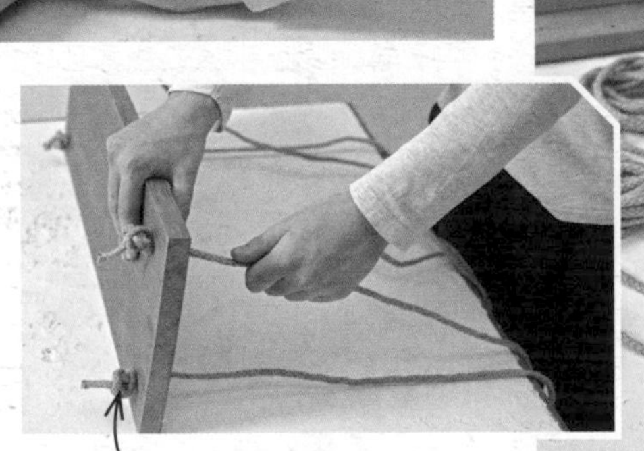

The four knotted ends of cord should all be on the underside of the shelf.

2 Cut the sash cord into four equal lengths of 2m (6ft), or longer if you have a high ceiling. Tie a double knot securely at the end of one length of cord, thread the other through one hole in the shelf, and pull the cord tight. Repeat with the other three lengths of cord.

3 To calculate how much space you require between shelves, measure the height of your plants and add a little extra room for growth. Pull one cord taut and mark this measurement on it with a clothes peg. Repeat with the other cord lengths.

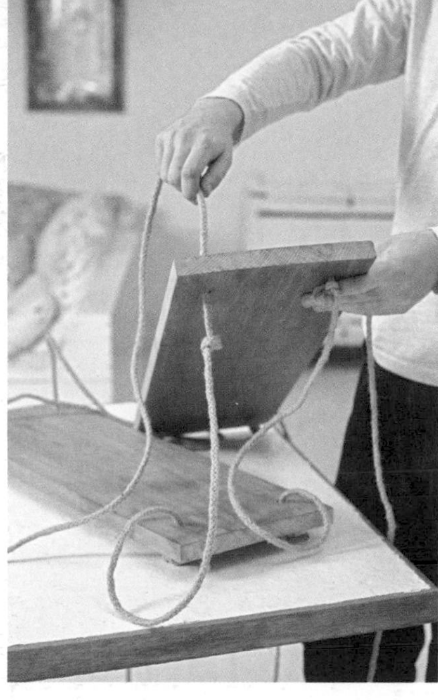

4 Make a knot just above each clothes peg and thread the lengths of cord through the holes of the second piece of wood. Adjust the knots if the top shelf doesn't hang level.

5 Plant up the herbs into plastic pots with drainage holes using multi-purpose compost mixed with a handful of vermiculite. Place these pots in lightweight ornamental waterproof containers.

Caring for tea herbs

Water the plants every two to three days, ensuring the compost doesn't become waterlogged - tip any excess water out of the decorative pots if this occurs. Feed with an all-purpose fertilizer for leafy crops every two weeks. Harvest the leaves no more than once a week; if any stems start to die off, cut them out. More shoots should then appear at the base.

Place one potted herb in the centre of each shelf first, then add other pots to prevent the shelf tipping up.

6 Make a loop in the top of each length of cord with another secure knot. To suspend the shelves, hang each loop from a sturdy hook fixed to a crossbeam in the ceiling by a window. Place the potted herbs on the shelves, ensuring their weight is evenly distributed so the shelves hang level.

Water herbs every 2-3 days

Orchids on bark create an eye-catching wall display. If the stems of the orchid plant start to stretch towards the light, try moving the display to the opposite wall.

Edible orchids mounted onto bark

Level 2 moderate

Dendrobiums are a group of edible orchids that taste like a mix of kale and cucumber. They make colourful **cake decorations** – or try battering and frying them like **tempura**. They can be grown in pots or some, like 'Berry Oda', can be **fixed to bark** and displayed on a wall (see project overleaf).

Choosing dendrobiums

There are many types of dendrobium, and although all the flowers are edible, some people are allergic to them, so try a tiny piece first to ensure you don't have a reaction. Check individual plant labels for specific care tips, since different types of dendrobium require different conditions. Many like a cool environment in winter and warmth in summer, and all grow best in bright but not direct sunlight. To crystallize the flowers for cake decorations, paint with beaten egg white, then dust with caster sugar. Leave the sugared blooms to dry for about 24 hours.

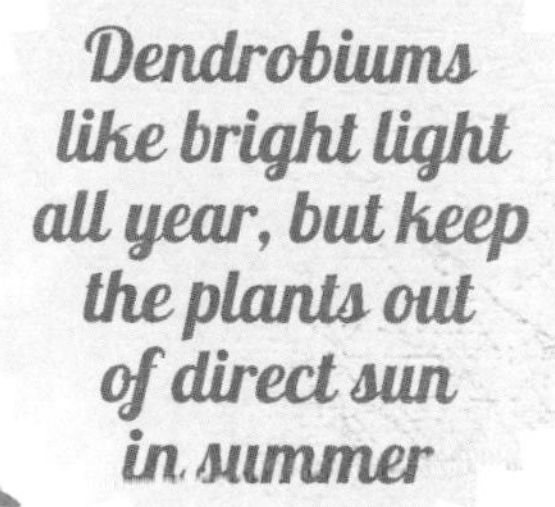

Orchid cake decoration

Dendrobiums like bright light all year, but keep the plants out of direct sun in summer

Named varieties
Orchids such as this 'Berry Oda' have been specially bred for growing in centrally heated homes. Like all dendrobiums, however, they still require high humidity and good ventilation.

Phalaenopsis type
These dendrobiums are evergreen and flower two to three times a year. They enjoy warmth in summer, but prefer lower temperatures and less watering between flowering periods.

Nobile type
Nobile dendrobiums flower in summer. They prefer warm temperatures in summer and cooler, drier conditions in winter; if pot-grown, allow the top of the compost to dry out between waterings.

Quick growing guide

1-2 hours to mount on bark

Likes bright light. Temperature depends on season and orchid variety

Water every two days in summer; once a week in winter

Feed weekly with a proprietary orchid fertilizer

Cut flowers when needed

Project

Mount an edible orchid onto bark

A small-flowered, **compact** dendrobium with delicate, sweetly scented flowers is perfect for mounting onto bark for a wall display. Hang it in a **bright spot** near a window, and **mist** it once a day. It will also need **watering** a few times a week.

It's best to mount your orchid when it is not in flower, which will cause the plant less stress as it adapts to its new home

YOU WILL NEED

- small dendrobium orchid, such as 'Berry Oda'
- coat hanger or short length of wire bent into a hook at one end
- sharp scissors or secateurs
- piece of cork bark or tree bark (available online); a piece of slate is also an option
- small bag of sphagnum moss
- small roll of transparent fishing line
- small roll of medium-gauge wire for the mount
- screwdriver
- screw or small picture hook for wall
- mist sprayer
- bucket

Use this method to mount dendrobiums on pieces of slate for a different look

1 Water the plant a few hours before transplanting it. Knock it out of its pot onto a clean surface. If you suffer from any plant allergies, wear gloves to handle the orchid. Using the coat hanger, gently remove the compost from the roots. Take your time to tease out all the compost to leave the roots as clean as possible.

2 Using a pair of sharp, clean scissors or secateurs, carefully trim the orchid roots so they measure about 10cm (4in) in length. This will encourage new roots to form once the orchid has been mounted onto the bark. Also remove any dead growth or old stems from the upper part of the orchid.

3 Gently wrap the roots with damp sphagnum moss. Secure the moss in place with a length of fishing line. Make sure the line is not wrapped too tightly around the roots, as this could damage them.

4 Cut a long length of fishing line, tie one end of it around the bark, and knot it firmly to secure it. Leave the other end free to wrap around the orchid. Set the orchid onto the front of the bark and wrap the line around the moss-covered rootball 2–3 times to fix the plant in place. Take care not to damage the plant.

5 Wrap a length of fishing wire firmly around the top section of the bark and secure it with a knot. Tie some wire to it at the back to form a loop. Or, make two small holes at the top of the bark with a screwdriver, thread wire through, and tie in a loop. Hang on a hook fixed to a wall in a bright room by a window.

Caring for your orchid

Your bark-mounted orchid will need to be misted with distilled water or rainwater every day from spring to autumn; mist it once every two to three days in winter. In spring and summer, give the roots a good drink at least twice a week by dunking the whole display in a bucket of water for 10–15 minutes. To feed the orchid, dilute orchid fertilizer at the recommended rate in the bucket of water first before submerging the roots. Leave to drain on a draining board before hanging it up again. In winter, move it to a cool room and water it once a week; a temperature of 10–13°C (50–55°F) is ideal.

Watering a bark-mounted dendrobium

Edible flowers

Multiple varieties

A surprising number of flowers are edible, and offer a wide range of delicate flavours and colours. Use this selection to add a sparkling note to salads and cake decorations, or include them in any dish as a garnish.

How to grow

When to buy or sow

Buy flowers when they are in season, from spring to summer. Violas and pansies include spring/summer- and winter-flowering varieties, which together will supply you with blooms year-round.

Light & heat

All these flowers need a sunny spot to bloom well. Spring flowers last longer in cool conditions, while summer flowers thrive in warmer temperatures.

Watering

Keep all edible flowers well watered, but guard against waterlogging, which will cause many to rot.

Aftercare

Feed flowers weekly with a high potash fertilizer unless you are using a compost already enriched with plant food.

Harvesting

Remove the flower and its stalk when the blooms have fully opened. Picking the blooms frequently encourages more flowers (apart from tulips) to form.

Varieties to try

There are many delicately flavoured edible flowers, but these are among the best for growing indoors. Check the plant labels first for more specific care advice on those flowers you wish to grow.

BELLIS DAISY ♥
Bellis perennis
These spring flowers are cousins of the common lawn daisy, and you can use the petals as a colourful garnish on desserts or soups, or in salads. Do not eat these flowers if you are a hayfever sufferer, though, as they may trigger an allergic reaction.

PANSY ♥
Viola species
The pretty blooms of both pansies and dainty violas have a delicate lettuce-like flavour and there are even varieties that flower in the winter months. The flowers can be crystallized and used on cakes, cookies, and desserts, or use the fresh petals on salads.

TULIP ♥
Tulipa species
Tulip petals have a surprisingly sweet, pea-like flavour, but some people have a strong allergic reaction to them, so take care before sampling. The most flavoursome are the single, early-flowering tulips. Never eat the bulbs, which are poisonous.

Colourful gems

Tulip petals make pretty canapés when topped with a little beetroot or goat's cheese dip. **Add colour** to your pancakes by sprinkling pansy petals onto the batter during cooking. **Pair violas** with primroses and scatter the blooms over lightly dressed iceberg lettuce leaves for a delicately flavoured salad.

To crystallize edible flowers such as violas and dendrobium orchids, use a clean paintbrush to cover the petals with whisked egg white, then dip in caster sugar and leave to dry for about 24 hours until hard (see also p53). **Scatter** primrose petals over a salad of lettuce leaves, cucumber, walnuts, grapes, and goat's cheese to add colour and flavour.

Decorative crystallized orchids on a cake

PRIMROSE ♥
Primula species
This group of edible spring flowers includes polyanthus, cowslips, primroses, and primulas. All have a subtle sweet taste, and are ideal to crystallize for decorations for cakes and desserts. Remove the stalks before using the flowers.

LAVENDER ♥
Lavandula species
The aromatic flavour of lavender flowers complements both sweet and savoury dishes. Add them to a bag of sugar to enhance cakes and desserts, or pop a few blooms into a glass of sparkling wine or champagne. Lavender flowers also work well in meat dishes and in ice cream.

CARNATION ♥
Dianthus species
Pinks, sweet Williams, and carnations all fall into this edible flower category, and most have a spicy, clove-like flavour, especially the more fragrant varieties. Remove the white heel at the base of the petals before use, as this part of the flower tastes bitter.

Quick growing guide

2-3 hours to paint the ladder and pot up the plants

Bright sunny room 14-22°C (57-72°F)

Water every day or two

Six weeks after planting, feed weekly

Pick flowers as required

Edible flower ladder

Level 1 easy

Edible spring flower salad

Displaying **pots of edible flowers** on a short stepladder in a bright room is an effective way of ensuring they all receive enough **light and space** to thrive. Use a selection of different **seasonal blooms** to create variety and colour.

YOU WILL NEED • short wooden stepladder • sandpaper • undercoat and topcoat wood paint • paint brush • containers of various sizes and saucers, plus plastic pots • selection of edible flowers (pp56-57) • multi-purpose compost • old belt (optional) and adhesive putty • potash fertilizer

1 Sand down the stepladder, apply one coat of undercoat, and allow to dry. Add one or two coats of emulsion paint, allowing the first coat to dry thoroughly if you add a second coat.

Cover the undercoat with emulsion in a colour that matches your interior decor.

2 Choose short-stemmed flowering plants that will sit comfortably on the steps. Select pots with drip trays or planters without drainage holes at the bottom. If using the latter, plant the flowers in plastic pots that can then be slipped inside them. Use multi-purpose compost to pot up the plants. Secure longer pots with an old belt or thick twine.

3 Secure the bases or saucers of the smaller containers to the steps with adhesive putty. Keep the plants well watered, checking on them daily. After six weeks, start feeding the flowers with a liquid potash fertilizer using a watering can with a fine rose head.

The flavour of edible herb flowers such as chives and lavender is similar to their leaves
Primroses need good drainage to prevent mildew disease.
Violas and pansies will flower for several weeks.
For a lavender plant, choose a large container with a drip tray.
Taller plants can be displayed next to the ladder.
Water small pots daily, but ensure they do not become waterlogged.
Choose a wide range of seasonal edible flowers for an unusual but beautiful display that tastes as good as it looks.

Level 2
moderate

Grow **lemongrass** from shop-bought stems

An essential ingredient in many **Asian dishes**, this large, grass-like **tropical herb** can be grown indoors by rooting some fresh stems bought from the supermarket and growing them on in a **sunny room**.

Quick growing guide

1 hour for various stages

Full sun

Water every 3-4 days

Feed with balanced liquid fertilizer every 2 weeks

Harvest when the stems are mature

YOU WILL NEED • lemongrass stems • chopping board • sharp knife • glass or mug for water • small plastic pots • multi-purpose compost • large container for mature plants

1 Peel off the outer layer from each of the lemongrass stems. With a sharp knife, cut off the top half of the stems, and use these to flavour stir-fries and rice dishes.

2 Place the stems in a glass of clean water and leave in a bright area out of direct sun for a few weeks. You will then see tiny roots emerge from the base of the stems.

Take care not to damage the fragile roots when planting.

3 Fill some small plastic pots with multi-purpose compost. Make a hole in the centre and pop a rooted stem in each. Firm gently with your fingertips and water them in.

Caring for & harvesting lemongrass

Set the lemongrass plants in a bright, sunny room. Keep the compost moist, but not wet. Feed the plants every fortnight. Harvest when they are 45–60cm (18–24in) in height; cut whole stems and trim off the leafy tops.

4 Water regularly, and leaves will soon form. When the roots start to grow through the pots' drainage holes, repot into a larger container of multi-purpose compost.

Set sun-loving plants on the top shelf of the trolley and mint on the bottom. Attach hanging planters of trailing strawberries and cucamelons to the handles.

Cocktail herbs & fruits

Impress your friends by serving **cocktails** made with fresh, homegrown ingredients, such as **mint**, **cucamelons**, **hyssop**, and **strawberries**, from a customized **cocktail trolley**. The trolley makes a practical plant stand and helps to create an attractive decorative display (see project overleaf).

Displaying your cocktail crops

A trolley makes the perfect plant stand for this range of potted herbs, edible flowers, and fruit. The cucamelons and hyssop (*Agastache*) should be placed on the top shelf or sunniest section of the trolley, while strawberries and mint, which grow happily in lower light conditions, will thrive on the lower shelf or in a container with hooks that can hang from one of the handles. If you don't own a trolley or haven't the space for one, a large windowsill, or home-made hanging shelves (p48), will work equally well.

Move the trolley around every few days to ensure your plants receive light on all sides

Cocktail herb & fruit options

Grow your favourite herbs to add to cocktails; search online for drinks recipes that include fresh herbs (or look on p65). Limes, strawberries, and cucamelons also make delicious cocktail ingredients and garnishes.

Cucamelons
These tiny watermelon lookalikes taste like cucumber with a hint of lime; blend the fruits or use as a garnish (see pp157–59 for growing instructions).

Strawberries
Choose an everbearing variety that will produce fruits all summer (see pp172–73 for varieties and growing instructions).

Try adding strawberries to a daiquiri cocktail made with rum.

Mint
Peppermint and spearmint are most frequently added to cocktails, but there are many other varieties you can try too (see pp66–67).

Quick growing guide

3-4 hours for various stages

Full sun or part shade

Water every 2-3 days

Feed weekly when fruit flowers appear with high potash fertilizer; fortnightly for herbs with fertilizer for leafy crops

Harvest when fruits are ripe; snip herb leaves as required

Project >>

Planting herbs & fruits for a cocktail trolley

Grow some **herbs**, **flowers**, and **fruits**, such as those listed here, to make the **cocktails you most enjoy** drinking. You can even add to the cocktail theme by dressing your trolley with edibles in planters made from **ice buckets** and **drinks trays**.

Hyssop and mint will grow on from year to year so store them in a cool area in winter

YOU WILL NEED

- cocktail trolley
- 1 hyssop plant
- 3-4 small mint plants in pots with drainage holes (see pp66-67for varieties and growing instructions)
- 3 everbearing strawberry plants, in plastic pots with drainage holes (see pp169-73 for varieties and growing instructions)
- 2-3 cucamelon plants, in plastic pots with drainage holes (see pp157-59 for growing instructions)
- soil-based compost, such as John Innes no 2
- horticultural grit
- multi-purpose compost
- plastic pots
- ice bucket and trough
- 2 hanging, or wall, waterproof planters with hooks attached
- gold spray paint for metal surfaces (optional)
- watering can fitted with rose head

1 Start by planting up the hyssop, which likes very well-drained compost. Water the plant well and set to one side to drain. Combine a 70:30 mix of soil-based compost and horticultural grit.

2 Add some of the compost and grit mix to a large plastic pot that fits inside an ice bucket. Set the potted plant on top of the compost and check that once planted it will sit 1-2cm (½-¾in) below the rim.

3 Tip the hyssop out of its pot and plant it in the larger container, filling the space around the rootball with the compost/grit mix, and pressing it down gently to remove any air gaps.

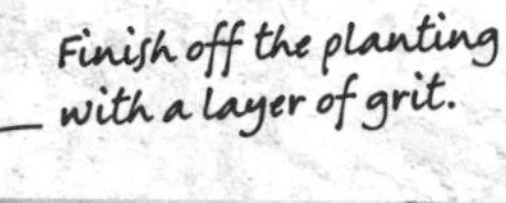

4 Water the plant well. Then add a layer of grit over the compost to act as a mulch (see p201), which is both decorative and helps retain moisture in the compost.

5 Spray the base of the ice bucket in a well-ventilated area with a gold spray. Leave to dry, then place the potted hyssop inside it and set it on top of the trolley.

6 Water each mint in its plastic pot and set aside to drain. Spray the trough, allow to dry, then set the pots of mint in the trough on the lower shelf at the front.

7 Water the cucamelons in their own plastic pots, allow to drain, and set them inside a long waterproof planter with fixed hooks. Hang the planter by its hooks over the handle at one end of the trolley, taking care not to tip the trolley up.

8 Water the everbearing strawberry plants in their pots, set them inside a second long waterproof planter with fixed hooks, and attach it to the other side of the trolley. Keep all the plants well watered, checking that none become waterlogged.

Cocktail recipe ideas

Strawberry Martini

Blitz a few handfuls of strawberries in a blender and add a splash of vermouth and gin, or vodka, to taste. Blitz for a few more seconds with some ice and serve with a strawberry and cucamelon garnish.

Mint & cucamelon Pimm's

Fill a jug with Pimm's and lemonade, stir and add ice, mint sprigs, and halved strawberries and cucamelons.

Herb- and fruit-infused cocktails

Mint

Mentha species

One of the easiest herbs to grow, mint thrives in part shade and requires little aftercare, but it spreads quickly. To prevent it swamping other herbs, plant it in a pot of its own.

Trailing mint stems can grow up to 1 metre (3 ft) in length.

Peppermint (Mentha x piperita) has a rich, fresh flavour, and can be used for teas and in savoury dishes.

Peppermint

How to grow

When to buy or sow

Mint is a deciduous herb that dies down over winter. Buy young plants in spring or early summer and repot into larger containers using multi-purpose compost to give them space to grow. This will also ensure they produce a plentiful supply of leaves.

Light & heat

Best in semi-shade and a cool situation, mint will also cope with more sunlight and warmer conditions if watered frequently. Rotate plants every few days to achieve balanced growth, and make sure your home is well ventilated in summer.

Watering

Mint requires watering when the top of the compost is just drying out. It's worth checking that your pots have adequate drainage to prevent the plants from developing fungal diseases.

Aftercare

Depending on the variety, mint can grow up to 60cm (24in) or taller, so give your plants plenty of headroom. If the leaves start to look dull or lose their colour after a couple of months, apply an all-purpose fertilizer every week or two.

Harvesting

Allow your mint to reach 30cm (12in) in height before harvesting. You can then remove the stem tips with about three pairs of leaves on each.

Basil mint

BASIL MINT ▶
(Mentha x *piperita* f. *citrata* 'Basil'*)*
This mint combines traditional peppermint and basil flavours and will enhance a range of savoury dishes. Try it in a pesto for pasta instead of basil.
Height: 60cm (2ft)

◀ INDIAN TRAILING MINT
(Satureja douglasii)
Not strictly a true mint, the stems of this evergreen herb can grow up to a metre (3ft) or more in length. It is perfect for a hanging pot, and tastes like garden mint.

Best indoor varieties

There are hundreds of varieties of mint to choose from, ranging from the bright tangy flavours of common garden mint (peppermint), through to those with hints of chocolate, basil, grapefruit, and apple scents. Some mint plants also sport colourful leaves, such as the black-leaved peppermint and variegated pineapple mint, and all varieties can be grown indoors.

▲ PINEAPPLE MINT
(Mentha suaveolens 'Pineapple'*)*
With a hint of pineapple flavour, this variety of mint is ideal for desserts and puddings, or add it to a fruit salad for extra zing. It has decorative variegated leaves. **Height:** 20-30cm (8-12in)

▲ CHOCOLATE MINT
(Mentha x *piperita* f. *citrata* 'Chocolate'*)*
A rich peppermint flavour combined with a chocolate scent makes this an excellent choice for teas and desserts. It is a compact variety of mint with attractive dark foliage. **Height:** 30-45cm (12-18in)

▲ APPLE MINT
(Mentha suaveolens)
Tangy and fresh, this mint is perfect for lamb dishes, or add it to peas and potatoes. A tall variety with bright green leaves and a delicious scent. **Height:** up to 90cm (36in)

▲ LIME MINT
(Mentha x *piperita* f. *citrata* 'Lime'*)*
The leaves of this refreshing mint have a lemony lime aroma and work well in fish and chicken dishes, as well as in hot or cold teas and cocktails. **Height:** 40cm (16in)

Easy propagation

You can make new mint plants for free simply by removing a few stems from one of your existing plants and popping them in water. When you see roots appear, pot up the stems in some multi-purpose compost. Keep the compost moist and they will soon sprout more stems and leaves.

Cook's tips

Versatile mint

Add a sprig to potatoes or peas as they boil.
Include a few leaves in ice cream and fruit salads.
Make refreshing fresh mint tea to help soothe stomach upsets and aid digestion.
For a sauce for lamb dishes, finely chop peppermint leaves, put in a bowl, add a teaspoon of sugar and some boiling water, leave to cool, drain off most of the water, and add vinegar to taste.
Roll cubes of feta cheese in a mix of finely chopped mint, chives, and cumin seeds. Thread each cheese square onto a skewer with a cube of cucumber, a black olive, and a single mint leaf (below).

Minty canapés

Create a focal point with a variety of hanging herb pots suspended at different heights – just ensure you can reach them all to water and feed the plants.
Hang your jars close to a sunny window and turn them every few days for the best results.
Use vases as table pots for herbs, such as pineapple sage, that will grow tall.
Mint will need a large jar to grow well.

Herbs in hanging jars

If you don't have a sunny windowsill on which to set herbs (pp36–39), try **growing** them in **hanging jars or vases** suspended close to a window from **hooks** in the ceiling (see project overleaf).

Keeping herbs happy

These hanging jars are quite straightforward to make, but check that the containers are large enough to comfortably fit your chosen herb plants. You can paint the bottoms in a colour to suit your decor and hang them at different heights to create a dynamic display. Twist the herb jars around every few days to ensure the plants' stems grow evenly.

Small, young thyme, mint, sage, and basil plants are ideal for planting in hanging jars

Alternative containers

Any glass or plastic pot with a wide neck that is more than 18cm (7in) deep can be transformed into a herb hanging container. Vigorous plants, such as mint, will be happier in a larger pot, and if weight is an issue, choose a plastic item from the mixed selection of containers below.

Household items such as plastic bowls, jars, tin buckets, and even large beer glasses can be transformed into hanging containers. Simply follow the steps overleaf.

Quick growing guide

2 hours, plus drying time for paint

Full sun 10-22°C (50-72°F)

Water when the top of the compost feels dry

Feed every 2-4 weeks with a fertilizer for leafy crops

Snip leaves as required during growing season

Project >>

Make hanging jars for herbs

Choose a container that is **deep enough** to accommodate your herb plant and one that has an area at the base for **water to drain** into. **Hang the jars** in plant holders made from electrical cable for a contemporary look, or try using jute rope for a more rustic design.

Water the herbs every few days when the top of the compost feels dry, but don't overwater them

YOU WILL NEED

- glass vessel, such as a large jam jar or vase, with a neck approx 18cm (7in) wide
- 10m (33ft) or more of plastic-coated electrical cable wire (available from DIY stores) or jute rope
- metal washer or ring
- paint for glass (or plastic, depending on your choice of container - see p69)
- handful of polystyrene packaging, broken into pieces, per pot
- horticultural grit
- selection of small herb plants (see pp40-41, 46-47, 66-67, 72-73, 74-75)
- soil-based compost, such as John Innes no 1
- large sturdy screw-in hooks, or hang the pot from a curtain pole

1 Cut four lengths of electrical cable (or rope) at least 1.5m (5ft) long, or longer if you have high ceilings. A 1.5m cable will suspend the jar about 65cm (26in) from the ceiling. Fold the cable in half and slip the folded end through the washer to form a loop (left). Then thread the two ends of the cable through the loop (below).

2 Pull the cable back towards you and tighten it. Repeat this process for the remaining three lengths of cable to form the base of the plant holder.

3 Paint the bottom of the jar using glass paint. A wavy edge creates the impression it has been dipped. Apply two coats and allow to dry between each coat.

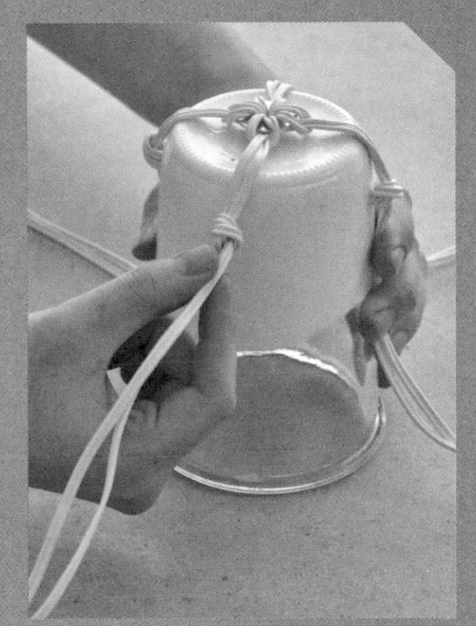

4 Turn the jar upside down. Fit the cable-washer base over the bottom of the jar and make four simple knots in each set of cables around the sides, as shown.

5 Separate the cables in two of the sets. Knot two adjacent single cables together at the top of the jar. Repeat with the other three sets of cables.

6 Remove the jar. Add some small pieces of polystyrene to create a well at the bottom for drainage (see p28). Add a layer of horticultural grit on top, and then some soil-based compost on top of the grit.

7 Water the herb, and slip it out of its original pot. Place in the jar and fill around the edges with more compost. Check that there are no gaps and then firm the compost gently with your fingertips.

8 Set the jar in the plant holder and tie all the ends together at the top. Hang on a hook secured firmly to a joist in the ceiling or a curtain pole. Water the herbs sparingly when the top of the compost feels dry.

Oregano & parsley

Origanum vulgare & Petroselinum crispum

These decorative herbs will grow both in full sun or part shade, and make good pot plants for an indoor kitchen windowsill. The nutrient-rich leaves offer distinctive flavours, ideal for a wide range of hot and cold savoury dishes.

To harvest the herbs, simply break off the tips of the stems.

Oregano (left), also commonly known as marjoram, and curly-leaved parsley

How to grow

When to buy or sow

Oregano is a perennial, while parsley is a biennial, producing leaves in the first year and flowers in the second. Both can be bought as young plants in spring; repot in a container one or two sizes larger in a 3:1 mix of soil-based compost, such as John Innes no 1, and horticultural grit.

Light & heat

These herbs will be happy on a windowsill, but need watering more frequently if kept in full sun. Open windows during hot weather to increase ventilation. They also tolerate cold winter nights.

Watering

Both plants like good drainage and will suffer in wet soil, so only water when the top of the compost feels dry. Planting in pots with drainage holes and setting them on saucers helps avoid waterlogging.

Aftercare

Feed from spring to early autumn with all-purpose liquid fertilizer for leafy crops. Oregano dies down in winter, but reshoots again in spring; repot it if the roots are congested. Only use parsley in its first year, as the leaves can taste bitter in the second.

Harvesting

Remove the stem tips from late spring to early autumn, taking just a few sprigs a time; removing too many stems will weaken the plant.

Oregano varieties

There are variegated and golden-leaved varieties, as well plain green, and all look pretty spilling over the sides of a pot. Oregano complements the flavours of fish and meat.

GOLDEN OREGANO ▶
(*Origanum vulgare* 'Aureum')
The bright yellow leaves are joined by pink flowers in summer, and both are edible. Add them to pizzas and pasta dishes, or use as a colourful garnish.
Height & spread: 45 x 45cm (18 x 18in)

SWEET MARJORAM ▲
(*Origanum majorana*)
This is traditional marjoram, and the green foliage has a slightly sweeter taste than other forms of oregano. Sprinkle the fresh leaves on meat and fish before or after cooking.
Height & spread:
45 x 60cm (18 x 24in)

VARIEGATED OREGANO ▶
(*Origanum vulgare* 'Country Cream')
Distinctive white and green variegated leaves and a slightly smaller stature set this variety apart from other forms. Use sprigs as a garnish or add roughly chopped leaves to a salad.
Height & spread:
30 x 30cm (12 x 12in)

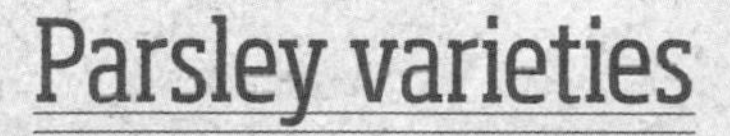

Parsley varieties

Parsley, of which there are two main types, makes the perfect garnish for almost any savoury dish, and combines particularly well with garlic and onions.

CURLY-LEAVED PARSLEY ▶
(*Petroselinum crispum*)
Curly-leaved French parsley has a mild flavour, and is used to enhance white fish dishes.
Height & spread:
40 x 40cm (16 x 16in)

FLAT-LEAVED PARSLEY ▶
(*Petroselinum crispum* var. *neapolitanum*)
This flat-leaved Italian type has a stronger flavour than its French cousin.
Height & spread:
60 x 60cm (24 x 24in)

Cooking with oregano

Sprinkle oregano leaves over a home-made tomato and mozzarella pizza.

Slice beefsteak and yellow tomatoes and roast with lemon wedges and oregano.

Cooking with parsley

Create a persillade of chopped parsley, crushed garlic, and seasoning, and stir into slow-cooked dishes.

Dress some fresh parsley leaves with lemon juice and zest, walnut oil, honey, sesame oil and seeds for a flavoursome side salad.

Try cooking a dish of *raki soslu barbunya*: Turkish red mullet seasoned with raki, lemons, and parsley.

Raki soslu barbunya

Sage & rosemary

Salvia species & Rosmarinus officinalis

These woody-stemmed, evergreen shrubby herbs both produce tasty leaves that can be harvested year after year from spring to autumn. Use them in meat and vegetable dishes to enliven the flavours.

Feed the herbs regularly to prevent the leaves turning yellow.

Common sage & rosemary

How to grow

When to buy or sow

Sage and rosemary are best grown from young plants, which are available all year. Tip them out of their pots and if the roots look very congested, repot in containers that are one or two sizes larger using a soil-based compost, such as John Innes no 1, mixed with horticultural grit for added drainage.

Light & heat

These herbs thrive in full sun on a windowsill. They prefer warmth in summer, and a slightly cooler but bright location in winter. Open the windows from spring to early autumn to increase ventilation.

Watering

Both are happiest in pots with holes in the bottom so water drains away freely. Water only when the top of the compost feels dry and never allow them to sit in soggy soil, which may cause them to rot.

Aftercare

Feed every two weeks from spring to early autumn with an all-purpose liquid fertilizer for leafy crops. As these plants will live for more than a year, repot them in spring in a 3:1 mix of soil-based compost and horticultural grit.

Harvesting

Remove just a few stem tips at a time. Do not remove leaves during the winter when the plants don't grow much, as this will weaken them.

Best sage varieties

The more colourful sage varieties can be combined with flowers to produce decorative displays indoors, or set them on a windowsill. Sage is traditionally used for stuffing for pork, while varieties with blackcurrant or pineapple aromas make great additions to fruit salads.

'ICTERINA' ▶
(*Salvia officinalis* 'Icterina')
Attractive gold-splashed green leaves make a decorative display on a windowsill. Use the leaves as you would common sage.
Height & spread: 30 x 45cm (12 x 18in)

PURPLE SAGE ▲
(*Salvia officinalis* 'Purpurascens')
The dark purple leaves of this form make a good foil for the plain green variety and have a similar flavour, ideal for meat dishes and stuffing.
Height & spread: 60 x 60cm (24 x 24in)

◀ 'TRICOLOR'
(*Salvia officinalis* 'Tricolor')
A beautiful variety with cream-edged grey-green leaves, which are flushed with purple when young. It tastes the same as common sage.
Height & spread: 30 x 45cm (12 x 18in)

◀ COMMON SAGE
(*Salvia officinalis*)
The plain green variety of sage is the best choice for pork dishes and, of course, stuffing. The flowers are edible too.
Height & spread: 60 x 60cm (24 x 24in)

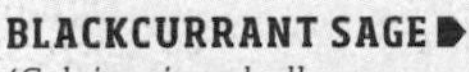

BLACKCURRANT SAGE ▶
(*Salvia microphylla* var. *microphylla*)
This pretty plant produces leaves with a blackcurrant aroma and striking cerise red flowers in summer. Use it to flavour cocktails.
Height & spread: up to 90 x 20cm (36 x 8in)

PINEAPPLE SAGE ▶
(*Salvia elegans* 'Scarlet Pineapple')
This tall form has spikes of scarlet summer flowers. Use the pineapple-scented leaves to flavour puddings and ice creams.
Height & spread: approx 90 x 45cm (36 x 18in)

Best rosemary varieties

The three main types of rosemary produce leaves with the same flavour, but each forms a slightly different shaped plant. Common rosemary (right) creates a vase-shaped shrub, Miss Jessopp's (*Rosmarinus officinalis* 'Miss Jessopp's Upright') has a slimmer, upright habit, and prostrate rosemary (*Rosmarinus officinalis* 'Prostratus') trails slightly.

COMMON ROSEMARY ▲
(*Rosmarinus officinalis*)
Typically used as an accompaniment to lamb, chicken, and game.
Height & spread: 60 x 40cm (24 x 16in)

Cooking with sage

Fry sage flower buds and leaves in butter, then mix in capers and lemon juice for a punchy pasta sauce.
Make a fruit salad with pineapple sage leaves, chopped kiwi, pineapple, banana and orange.
Roast butternut squash in olive oil for 40 minutes, then add sliced red onions and chopped sage leaves for a further 20 minutes.

Roast squash with sage

Cooking with rosemary

Roughly chop rosemary leaves, add with garlic cloves to a tray of potatoes, and roast slowly.
Add chopped rosemary leaves to a bolognese sauce and serve with fresh pasta.

Sprouts, leaves & roots

Packed with nutrients, most of these edibles are easy to grow. Sprouts and microgreens are ready to eat within a week or two; carrots and other roots take longer, but the flavour they offer in return is worth waiting for.

Introducing sprouts, leaves & roots

The crops in this group include some of the **quickest** and **easiest plants** to grow indoors, and provide a **consistent supply** of ingredients for your favourite dishes.

Shooting for the stars

Newly sprouted beans, peas, and seeds need no compost or special equipment, but the rewards are great for the indoor gardener, as these little nutrient bombs are bursting with flavour and packed with health-boosting vitamins, minerals, and antioxidants. They are all very easy to grow and will sprout within a few days in glass jars or special sprouting units, which are available to buy online.

Leafing through the menu

Growing your own salad leaves ensures the freshest taste, crispest texture, and highest vitamin content when you pluck them straight from the plant. If you're an impatient gardener or stuck for space, tiny microgreens offer a perfect solution, with varieties such as radish and broccoli ready to harvest in just a few weeks. Garlic shoots are another easy option for beginners; all you need is a garlic bulb or two and some little glasses to grow a crop of tangy leaves.

Down to the roots

You may be surprised to learn that a few of the most popular root crops, including carrots and radishes, can be grown indoors. And by growing your own from seed, you will have access to an array of varieties, such as purple carrots and white radishes, that are not available in shops. By controlling their growing environment you can also reduce the need for pesticides, enabling you to enjoy chemical-free crops. Root crops enjoy bright conditions in a room that won't get too hot, although if the temperature rises remember to water them every day or two.

Best zones for sprouts, leaves & roots

The majority of these crops require cool conditions, and are best grown in zones 2, 6, 7, and 8. They may struggle in warmer areas, and radishes, beetroot and salad leaves are likely to bolt (flower) more quickly.

South-facing windows
Most of these crops are too large for a windowsill and salad leaves will struggle in full sun and the intense heat. Spring onions and chives may thrive here if watered well.

East- and west-facing windows
A better option for salad leaves, microgreens, and sprouts, these cooler locations offer plants plenty of light with less heat than zone 1. Water well to prevent crops drying out.

Beneath a skylight
These plants will perform well under a skylight from autumn to spring, but the room may become too hot in summer. Water plants regularly to prevent wilting.

Walls
You can grow sprouts in jars and microgreens on shelves fixed to bright walls; turn the latter every day so they don't grow spindly. Mushrooms will also grow on a shelf.

Dark corners
Leafy crops, spring onions, radishes, and round carrots can all be grown under domestic grow lights in dark corners; mushrooms require no additional light here.

Centre of a room
All crops will be happy in the middle of bright room, as long as it is not too hot. Microgreens, salad leaves, and mushrooms grow in rooms that don't receive direct sun.

Cool (unheated) south-facing room
All crops will enjoy the bright but cool conditions here. Some seeds may struggle to germinate in spring in an unheated room, but should grow well once sprouted.

Outside windowsill
These crops are all reasonably hardy and will grow well on an east- or west-facing sill; a north-facing sill may work for salad crops. Sprouts are best grown indoors.

Quick growing guide

3 minutes to prepare; leave overnight to soak

Keep out of direct sun 18-21°C (64-70°F)

Rinse 2-3 times a day

No need to feed

Use the seeds as soon as they sprout

Level 1 easy

Sprouts in jars

Easy to grow, these **seeds and dried beans** will spring into life after just a few days to make **nutritious sprouts** that can be used in a range of fresh salads, stews, curries, and savoury smoothies and juices.

Mung beans sprouted in a dark place will have fewer nutrients than those grown in the light

YOU WILL NEED • seeds or beans, sold for sprouting (see pp82-83 for ideas) • Kilner or wide-mouthed jam jars • fine sieve or strainer • muslin • elastic band (if using jam jars)

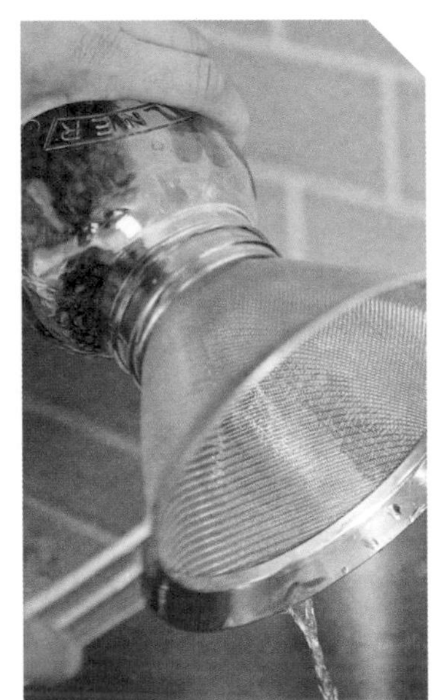

1 Place the seeds (or beans) in a Kilner or jam jar so that it is less than a quarter full. Fill the jar with cold water and leave the seeds to soak overnight. They will swell and expand as they absorb the water.

2 Drain the seeds well using a sieve or strainer as shown (above) so they remain in the jar. Keep the seeds moist, which enables them to sprout, but not wet, as this can lead to potentially harmful fungal diseases. Stand the jar out of direct sunlight, ideally near a kitchen tap to make rinsing the seeds more convenient.

3 In between rinsings, place a piece of muslin over the jar and secure with the Kilner screw-top or an elastic band. Rinse your seeds at least twice a day until little shoots appear. Then rinse and strain the sprouts. Tip onto a paper towel to dry before using.

Buy sprouting seeds and beans from a specialist supplier for a cornucopia of flavours and textures
Muslin or cloth prevents insects and dust from spoiling your sprouts.
Sprouts are ready as soon as the seeds or beans form little shoots.
Sprouts can be stored for up to a week in the fridge after they have germinated. Rinse thoroughly once again in fresh water before using.

Sprouts

Multiple varieties

They may be tiny, but sprouts are packed with nutrients, and add a delicious crunchy texture and flavour to savoury dishes such as stir-fries, salads, and sandwiches. They are the ultimate "fast food", growing in just a few days.

Most sprouts are ready to eat within days, making them the ultimate crop for impatient gardeners

How to grow

When to buy or sow

You can buy a variety of beans, seeds, and peas to sprout at any time of year.

Light & heat

To produce sprouts in Kilner or jam jars, use the method described on p80, or choose specially designed sprouting jars or units, which are available to buy online. Keep the jars or units in a bright place out of direct sunlight; most seeds and beans will sprout at 18–21°C (64–70°F).

Watering

Rinse in clean water twice a day until they have sprouted. This process normally takes just a few days under the right conditions.

Aftercare

These fast-growing crops need no aftercare, but do not leave them in the jars for more than a few days after they have sprouted.

Harvesting

When the sprouts are ready, rinse well and use immediately, or leave to dry on a paper towel for a few hours and store in a sealed container or sealed zip-lock bag in the fridge for up to a week. Discard any sprouts that show signs of mould or smell unpleasant.

Varieties

There is a huge choice of varieties available, ranging from mild alfalfa to curry-flavoured fenugreek. You will find the best selection from specialist suppliers online, some of which offer certified organic seeds and beans.

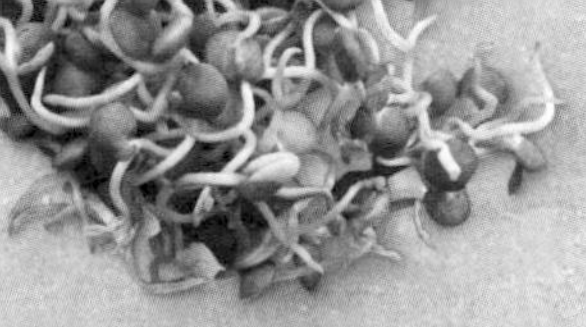

GREEN LENTILS
Nutty and mild in flavour, lentils are available in a range of colours. Sprouted lentils will complement most soups, salads and stews.

BROCCOLI
These intensely flavoured sprouts are packed with antioxidants. They prefer cool conditions, so incorporate an extra daily rinse in hot weather.

Nutrient boosts

You can add sprouts to almost any dish for a burst of flavour and nutrients; experiment to see which will complement your favourite recipes.

Add a few sprouts to the blender when you make a vegetable smoothie.

Use as a topping scattered over an omelette, in a sandwich, or inside a wrap.

Include a mix of sprouts in stir-fries and salads, or as a garnish on soups and pizza.

Make a fenugreek sprout curry or a chickpea sprout and vegetable stew.

Sprouts wrapped in a vine leaf

ALFALFA

One of the quickest seeds to sprout, alfalfa shoots have a mild taste with a pleasant texture that makes them ideal as a garnish and in sandwiches.

CHICKPEAS

Sprouted chickpeas are high in protein and so add both bulk and high levels of nutrients to a wide range of hot and cold dishes.

MUNG BEANS

Delicious in stir-fries and salads, the unique flavour and crunchy texture of mung beans makes them the most popular sprout in the world.

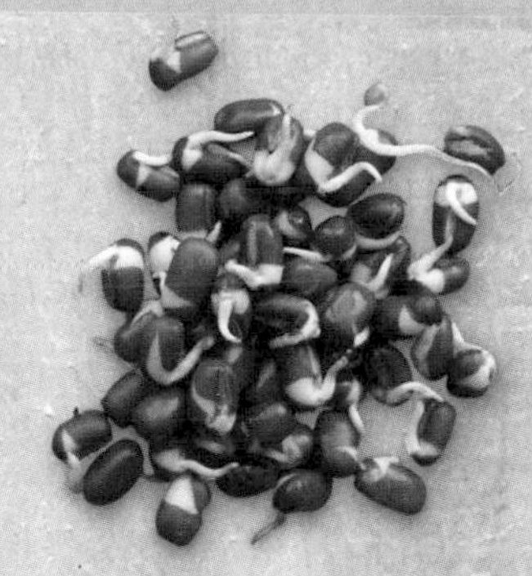

ADZUKI BEANS

Colourful and crunchy, adzuki beans have a delicate nutty flavour; ensure the white shoots are at least 1.5cm (½in) before eating the sprouts raw.

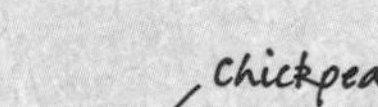

Level 1 easy

Microgreens in muffin cases

Packed with **nutrients** and exceptionally **easy to care for**, microgreens can be sown at any time of year in silicone muffin cases (see project overleaf), and placed on a **windowsill**. Once ready to harvest, display them as a pretty collection of **leafy cupcakes**.

What are microgreens?

These tiny flavoursome leaves are simply the young seedlings of edible plants that, given time, would grow into mature crops. Most take just two or three weeks to reach the stage when they are ready to eat, having formed a couple of sets of leaves. Research has shown that microgreens contain higher concentrations of nutrients than the mature plants, making them an attractive crop to grow.

Superfood nutrition
As they are picked and eaten almost immediately, none of the vitamins and antioxidants that microgreens contain are lost. Use them to add spice to salads and sandwiches, for example, or as a nutrient-rich garnish on savoury dishes.

Muffin cases make pretty yet practical containers for growing microgreens. When the microgreens are ready to eat, set them on a cake stand as a table centrepiece.

Use a pair of scissors to snip off the fresh microgreens just before you want to eat them

Quick growing guide

10 minutes to prepare and sow seeds

Sunny windowsill 14-22°C (57-72°F)

Water every day or two

No need to feed

Harvest when stems have 3-4 leaves

Project >>

Grow microgreens in muffin cases

Microgreen seeds need **warmth and light** to germinate, so you may find their shoots appear **more quickly** in spring and summer.

YOU WILL NEED • large silicone muffin cases • scissors • good-quality seed compost • vermiculite (optional) • selection of microgreen seeds • small watering can with fine rose head, or water bottle • tray that holds water • cake stand or large plate • microgreen snips (optional)

1 Fold the large muffin case in half (small muffin cases will work too, but the microgreen shoots need more watering as a result) and snip a hole in the base of the case with sharp scissors.

2 Fill the muffin case with good-quality seed compost to about 5mm (¼in) below the rim of the case. Firm the compost gently with your fingers to remove any air pockets.

3 Sow the seeds thickly and evenly on the compost, ensuring that they are all in contact with the surface and none are sitting on top of one another. Press them down lightly with your fingertips.

4 Cover the seeds with a thin layer of either compost or vermiculite (the latter allows light through and retains moisture). Repeat with different seeds in the remaining muffin cases.

Larger seeds, such as sunflowers, will require soaking overnight before sowing to ensure successful germination

5 Set the muffin cases on a tray, water the seeds gently with a watering can, and place the tray on a windowsill. Turn the cases every day so the stems grow evenly.

6 Water every day or two so that the compost is moist, but not wet. When ready, set the "cupcakes" on a cake stand or plate; snip off the shoots as needed.

Successional sowing

For a continuous harvest, either sow a batch of microgreen seeds in muffin cases or small pots every week, or sow seeds in larger pots for a bigger harvest. You can also sow seeds on one side of a wide pot one week, then sow on the other side the following week to extend the harvest period. Or, if you prefer, choose another variety to grow, which may have a shorter growing time and be ready to harvest around the same time that your first batch is ready. Turn the pot round every day or two so that both sides receive sufficient light. Use either of these techniques and you will have fresh microgreens to eat all year round.

Batch-sowing microgreens

Microgreens

Multiple varieties

A top crop for tiny indoor spaces, all you need to grow these diminutive leaves are a few small pots and a windowsill or sunny kitchen counter. Try growing a range of microgreens for different colours and flavours to pick fresh and add to your salads and sandwiches.

Radish & beetroot microgreens

How to grow

You can buy and sow microgreen seeds in small plastic pots or silicone muffin cases at any time of year, and most will germinate within a few days (see pp86–87 for more detailed growing tips). Keep your microgreens in a light area in full or part sun, and water the pots or cases every day or two. Harvest the young shoots when the stems have grown 2–4 leaves.

MICROGREEN SEEDS

VARIETY	HARVEST IN...
RADISH	12 DAYS
MIZUNA	12 DAYS
MUSTARD	14 DAYS
ROCKET	15 DAYS
BASIL	15 DAYS
BEETROOT	21 DAYS
AMARANTH	21 DAYS
FENUGREEK	21 DAYS
KALE	21 DAYS
CORIANDER	21 DAYS

Best varieties

Suppliers offer a special range of varieties labelled "microgreens", but you can use the more readily available ordinary seed packs for crops such as kale, beetroot, and basil, since they contain exactly the same seeds and will grow in the same way.

◀ BEETROOT
These colourful red stems, with leaves in green or red, taste similar to the sweet earthy roots, and help to brighten up salads and sandwiches.

RED AMARANTH ▲
Appearing almost luminous, these sparkling red leaves make a beautiful garnish for almost any dish. Packed with essential vitamins and minerals, the foliage tastes like lettuce.

KALE ▶
Milder in flavour than the dark green mature leaves, but with the same high nutrient content. Sprinkle kale microgreens onto soups or salads just before serving.

FENUGREEK ▶
The curry-like flavour of these little leaves will add a spicy kick to a sandwich, salad, or stir-fry. Fenugreek is also used in Asian cooking to aid digestion.

◀ RADISH
Available with red or green leaves, radish microgreens are among the fastest seeds to germinate and mature. Sprinkle the spicy seedlings over any hot or cold dish.

BASIL ▶
An easy way to enjoy fresh basil without the bother of growing a full-size crop, these young seedlings can be used in Mediterranean-inspired dishes.

MIZUNA ▲
The mild, slightly peppery taste of these pretty leaves adds depth to salads, and also makes a great topping for pasta and curry dishes.

◀ 'RED FRILLS' MUSTARD
These pink-red leaves inject mustard and horseradish flavours to salads, stir-fries and sandwiches, or use them as a colourful garnish.

Little leafy dishes

Sprinkle basil or mizuna microgreen leaves over tomato soup before serving.
Add a few different microgreens to an open-topped cheese toastie.
Increase the flavour of an omelette by scattering microgreens generously over the filling.
Blend mild microgreens with frozen peaches, ripe banana, spinach, and water for a healthy smoothie.
Make a salad of mixed microgreens, cubed blood orange, avocado slices, shredded carrot, and chopped walnuts.

Home-made tomato soup with basil

These wall shelves take up little space in a room yet provide a home for a wide selection of edibles growing under fluorescent lights.

Level 3 advanced

Transform your shelves into a mini greenhouse

An ideal solution if your home does not offer much natural sunlight, **fluorescent grow lights** can be used to create a micro-indoor greenhouse to increase the **range of crops** you will be able to grow. The lights are surprisingly easy to fix to a set of **ordinary shelves** (see project overleaf).

What is a grow light?

Grow lights, or propagation lights as they are also known, imitate the sun's rays, which plants need to mature. They are used widely in the horticultural and agricultural industries to aid plant growth in winter, but smaller units are available for domestic use. These are easy to fit to shelving, or you can buy propagation units with integral lights to raise seeds and young plants.

Before buying grow lights, compare the running costs of different types and brands

Crops to try

You can grow almost any crop under a grow light, but if using lights fixed to shelves, you will be limited to small plants that can fit on them. Shelves are perfect for growing vegetable seeds that need light to germinate, young seedlings, and other short-stemmed plants.

Salads & microgreens

Try growing microgreens and lettuces in long troughs that make the best use of the space on a shelf. The artificial light encourages seeds to germinate and enables you to grow these leafy crops all year round.

'Litte Gem' lettuce is a compact Cos variety.

Herbs

Many herbs, including coriander (shown), basil, oregano, and thyme, will fit on a shelf and do well with the help of a grow light.

Radishes

The seeds of small, fast-growing crops such as radishes and spring onions can be sown every few weeks to give continuous crops from late spring to autumn.

Quick growing guide

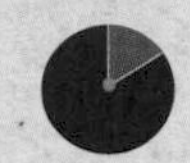
1-2 hours for various stages

Part sun for top shelves

Water every 2-3 days

Feeding depends on crops grown

Harvest lettuce and microgreens all year

Project >>

Create a **mini greenhouse**

Any set of **wooden shelves** can be used to create a **mini greenhouse** for growing plants (see also project overleaf), although the wider the shelves the better, as they will allow you to accommodate more plants. **Adjustable shelves** are a good idea if you want to grow taller crops.

Check that all your plant containers are waterproof so they don't leak onto the shelves or into the grow lights

YOU WILL NEED • set of wooden shelves • wood paint (optional) • single strip fluorescent grow light for each "greenhouse" shelf • pencil • ruler • a few plastic-coated wire ties • screwdriver & M10 80mm ($3^1/_8$ in) long screws to fix shelves to wall (if necessary)

Grow lights may have different attachment systems, so read the instructions before you start.

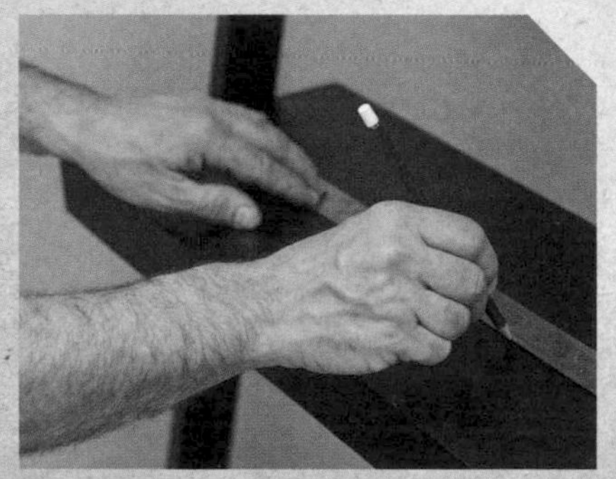

1 Turn the shelves upside down and secure them so they don't fall over. Using a pencil and ruler, measure the width of the underside of one of the shelves and draw a line lengthways through the centre.

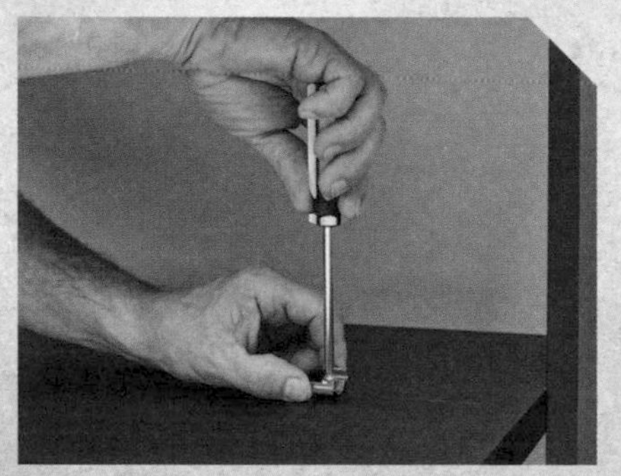

2 Centre the grow light unit along the pencil line marked on the shelf. Mark each end of the grow light with the pencil. Screw on the brackets supplied with the unit just inside these pencil marks.

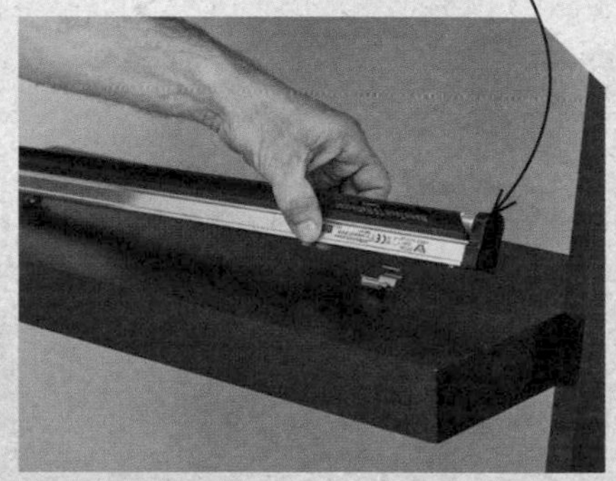

3 Repeat steps 1-2 for each shelf that requires a grow light. Then clip the lights on to their brackets, ensuring that the plug sockets on all the lights are facing the same side of the shelving unit.

4 When you have secured all the grow lights to the shelves, turn the unit back up the right way, and position it against a wall. Some units will need to be fixed to the wall with screws. Connect each light to its mains cable, as shown.

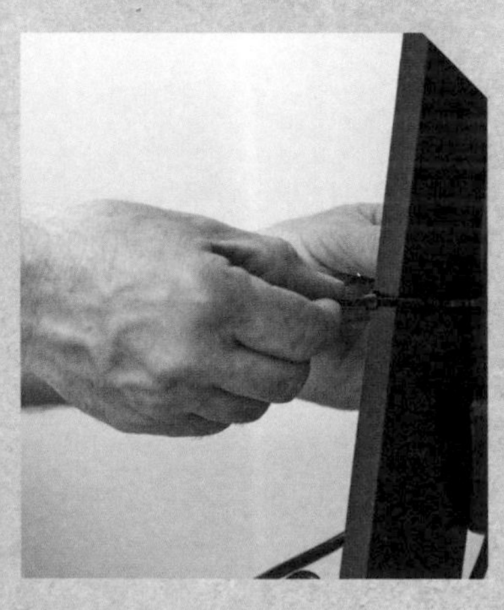

5 Secure the mains leads to the back of the shelving unit using plastic-coated wire ties. These will keep the leads tidy and prevent anyone from tripping on them. Once you have plugged the unit into the mains socket, you are ready to start growing crops.

6 You can display your shelves near a socket in a dark corner of the house, but if you set them close to or under a window or skylight that offers some supplementary sunlight, you can also make use of the top shelves to grow more crops.

Arranging your edibles

To provide your crops with sufficient light, the tops of the plants should sit just a few centimetres beneath the grow lights. If the plants are too far away, raise them up in their pots on glasses or other temporary supports. You can then remove the supports as the crops grow taller. Some grow lights are more powerful than others, so check first with your supplier to ensure you buy a product that is appropriate for your needs.

Raise up crops on upturned glasses

Project continues »

Raise lettuces from seed under grow lights

You can grow **lettuces** and similar leafy crops such as **mizuna** from seed in a long **shallow container** that will fit neatly onto a shelf fitted with a grow light, or on a bright windowsill out of direct sun.

YOU WILL NEED • long plastic container with drip tray • multi-purpose compost • bamboo cane • lettuce seeds • vermiculite • plant labels • watering can fitted with rose head • sharp scissors

Lettuces grow quickly from seed, and most will be ready to eat just six to eight weeks after sowing

1 If your container has no drainage holes, make a few small holes in the base. Fill with multi-purpose compost and press down gently to firm. Make two depressions lengthways in the compost with the bamboo cane.

2 Open the seed pack and tip some of the seeds into the palm of your hand. Using the forefinger and thumb of your other hand, sprinkle the seeds thinly along the two depressions. Cover the seeds with a thin layer of vermiculite. Place the container on its drip tray and label each container.

Thin congested seedlings when they are 2cm (¾in) tall.

3 Water the compost lightly and put the container on a shelf fitted with a grow light, placing it on supports if needed (p93). Keep the compost moist, but not wet. The seedlings will emerge within a week or two; once they are 5cm (2in) tall, thin them so they are about 2cm (¾in) apart.

Start feeding the seedlings when the leaves are about 10cm (4in) tall.

4 When the seedlings are 7cm (3in) tall, thin them again to about 7cm (3in) apart if you want full lettuce heads. Many multi-purpose composts are enriched with fertilizer, so your lettuces will not need any further feeding. If the compost you have used is not enriched, feed the plants when the leaves are 10cm (4in) tall with an all-purpose fertilizer for leafy crops.

5 If you are growing loose leaf lettuces, also known as cut-and-come-again types, harvest all the leaves by cutting them down to 4cm (1½in) stumps when they reach 15cm (6in) in height. The stumps will then reshoot to give a second crop.

If you have allowed your lettuces to develop into more fully formed heads, harvest them leaf by leaf from each plant as you need them. They will then grow more leaves.

Use sharp scissors to harvest cut-and-come-again varieties.

Pick individual leaves from fully formed lettuces as required.

Growing on a windowsill or under a skylight

You can also sow lettuce seed in pots to grow on a windowsill or under a skylight. Sow seed thinly in small plastic pots filled with multi-purpose compost, cover with vermiculite, and set in a bright place. Place the pots in pretty containers if you prefer an eye-catching display. Water the plants well, and thin the seedlings when they are 7cm (3in) tall, leaving 1–3 lettuces per pot (see steps 3 and 4) if you want full heads.

Lettuce under a skylight

Salad leaves

Lactuca sativa

Lettuce is the mainstay of any fresh salad or sandwich. There is a wide choice of varieties, particularly if you grow from seed, ranging from bitter to sweet in flavour and soft or crisp in texture.

Plant 1–3 lettuces in a 20cm (8in) pot and harvest leaf by leaf.

'Green Oak-Leaf' lettuce

How to grow

When to buy or sow

Lettuce seed is available throughout the year, or buy young seedlings in cell packs from a garden centre from spring to early summer. If you have a grow light (p91), sow seed in trays or pots of multi-purpose compost at any time of year. If not, sow every few weeks from early spring to early autumn. Lettuce germinates quickly and can be harvested within six to eight weeks from sowing.

Light & heat

Lettuce will not germinate above 25°C (77°F) and is most likely to succeed in cooler conditions, ideally below 21°C (70°F). Hot weather can also cause it to bolt (flower) early, which results in leaves with a bitter, unpleasant taste. Place your plants in a bright position out of direct sunlight.

Watering

Ensure plants are kept moist, but avoid waterlogged conditions, which may cause them to rot. Growing lettuces in a container with drainage holes, set on a drip tray, is the best way to avoid overwatering.

Aftercare

If you sow into seed compost, which contains few nutrients, feed after six weeks with diluted liquid fertilizer for leafy crops every fortnight. Delay feeding a little longer if you sowed into a multi-purpose compost, which contains more nutrients. (For harvesting lettuce leaves, see p95.)

Best salad leaf varieties

There are two main types of lettuce: those, such as Cos, that form a tight heart of closely packed leaves, and loose-leaf forms, often dubbed "cut-and-come-again" lettuces, because after cutting the leaf tops, the stubs regrow to offer a second harvest.

◀ COS LETTUCE
Cos, or romaine lettuces as they are also known, produce slender oval heads of tightly packed crisp leaves. Leave plants to develop into full-headed lettuces or harvest individual leaves when mature.
Height & spread:
25 x 10cm (10 x 4in)

'GREEN BATAVIAN' ▲
A frilly-leaved form, batavia lettuces have a nutty flavour and crisp texture. Thin the seedlings so they have space to develop into a loose head and harvest the whole plant when mature. **Height & spread:**
20 x 25cm (8 x 10in)

'LITTLE GEM' ▶
One of the earliest varieties to mature from a spring sowing, these small compact Cos-like lettuces produce crisp, sweet hearts. Thin the seedlings to allow individual plants to develop into heads.
Height & spread:
20 x 20cm (8 x 8in)

'LOLLO ROSSA' ▶
An Italian lettuce with a slightly bitter flavour, this decorative variety produces compact, loose heads of dark red frilly leaves. It can be used as a cut-and-come-again variety.
Height & spread: 15 x 25cm (6 x 10in)

'GREEN OAK LEAF' ▲
The frilly green leaves of this loose-leaf lettuce are sweet and soft in texture. Use as a cut-and-come-again variety, or harvest leaf by leaf when mature. Seedlings can also be thinned to allow plants to develop a loose head.
Height & spread: 20 x 25cm (8 x 10in)

◀ 'RED OAK LEAF'
The dark red leaves of this loose-leaf variety have a slightly bitter flavour, ideal for spicing up salads. Use it as a cut-and-come-again type or thin the seedlings and allow it to develop a frilly open head.
Height & spread:
20 x 25cm (8 x 10in)

Serving salad leaves

Wrap crispy duck or spiced chicken in crunchy Batavian lettuce leaves to create Chinese-inspired parcels.
Toss some Cos lettuce leaves into a vegetable stir-fry flavoured with chopped garlic and drizzled with sesame oil for a tasty dish with a difference.
Make a salsa verde using coarsely chopped loose-leaf lettuces combined with shallots, herbs, chillies, oil, and a pinch of citrus zest.
Add some sliced radishes and avocado to a bed of crisp lettuce leaves for a simple but refreshing side salad.
Serve a simple Caesar salad with a bed of fresh salad leaves topped with slices of chicken, cheese, and some croutons scattered on top.

Caesar salad

Cut out a segment of an old table and insert commercial metal serving dishes, which can be purchased online, in which to house your potted leafy salad crops.

Table-top spicy leaves

Try growing a range of **Asian-style leafy crops** inside metal serving dishes **set into your table top** to create a strikingly different display that's guaranteed to impress your dinner guests (see project overleaf).

Salads from seed

Asian leafy greens, such as Japanese mizuna, can all be bought as seedling plants from a garden centre, but they are easy to grow from seed too (see pp204–05). You will also find a wider choice of varieties if you buy from seed catalogues. These leafy greens will thrive in an area that is out of direct sunlight, so a dining room table can provide the ideal growing conditions.

Cool crops
Mizuna prefers a cool room and will need watering more frequently in hot weather.

Asian leafy crop options

You will find seeds for a wide range of nutrient-rich Asian greens from specialist seed merchants. Most grow well indoors from spring to autumn, and the crops require very little aftercare apart from frequent watering and an occasional dose of liquid fertilizer for leafy crops.

Pak choi
Choose from green- or purple-leaved varieties. Use the baby leaves in salads, or add full heads to stir-fries and soups.

Chop suey
For a long harvest, sow in pots fortnightly from spring to summer. Enjoy the tangy leaves in salads, soups and stir-fries.

Mibuna
Like its cousin mizuna, mibuna has a spicy flavour and is easy to grow from seed. Add to salads or steam lightly.

Quick growing guide

4 hours for various stages

Part sun

Water every day or two

Feed with liquid fertilizer for leafy crops

Harvest leaves as required

Create a **table top** for spicy **Asian leaves**

You will need just a few carpentry tools to **adapt an old wooden table**, or a piece of timber fixed onto trestle table legs, so you can **grow and display** a variety of **leafy greens** to pick as you need them for fresh salads or to stir-fry.

YOU WILL NEED • old wooden table or piece of timber • trestle table legs (if using timber) • stainless steel catering containers • pencil • ruler • electric screwdriver & bit • electric jigsaw • eye protectors & dust mask • sandpaper • plastic pots • gravel • multi-purpose compost • mizuna, mibuna, & pak choi seedlings

Look in your local secondhand and charity shops for an inexpensive wooden table to customize

1 Position the containers upside down in a line in the middle of the table and measure their width and length. Subtract the figures from the width and length of the table, and divide by two. Use these final measurements to ensure the containers are positioned centrally. Draw around their outer edges.

Draw around the edges of the containers with a pencil.

Make the rectangle slightly smaller than the trays.

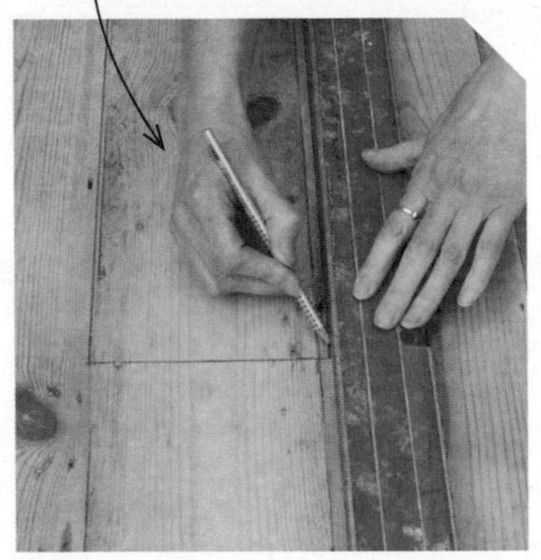

2 Draw a rectangle 5mm (1/4in) inside the pencil marks you have made around the trays. Once cut out, this slighty smaller hole will allow the trays to sit snugly in the table without falling through.

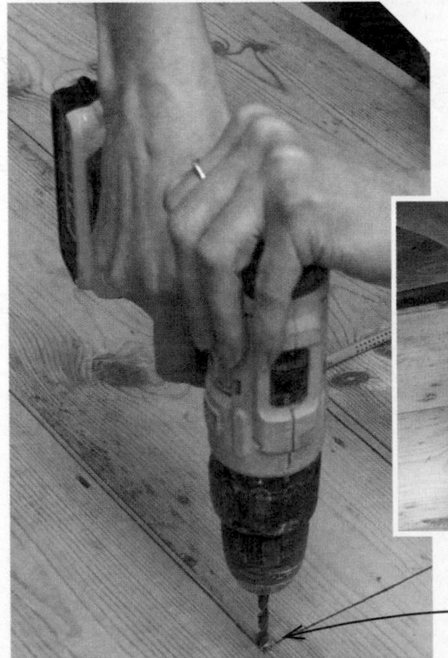

3 Make a hole in a corner of the rectangle for the jigsaw blade using a wood drill bit. Wearing eye protection and a dust mask, insert the blade and cut the wood.

Make an initial hole for the jigsaw blade.

Holding the jigsaw firmly, cut inside the pencil marks.

5 Check the plastic pots fit inside the containers, then plant them with mizuna, mibuna, and pak choi seedlings using multi-purpose compost. Add gravel to the bottom of the containers and pop the pots inside.

'Before sawing, check the width of the lip on the containers to ensure they won't fall through the table

4 Check that the containers fit inside the hole. If the hole is too small, sand down the edges until the containers will fit. Use the sandpaper to also smooth the edges and remove any splinters.

6 These crops like cool conditions out of direct sunlight. However, they will suffer in a dark corner, so position the table near a window or under a skylight. Turn the pots every day or two to ensure even growth, and water daily. Pick the leaves as required or leave the pak choi plants to develop full heads for frying or steaming.

Easy option

If you do not have a table to customize, grow some salad leaves in a colander. Line a large colander with plastic and add a coir hanging basket liner. Fill with multi-purpose compost and plant up your seedlings. Choose crops with different coloured leaves to make a decorative table-top display. Water every day or two, and turn the colander regularly to promote even growth.

Colander-grown salad leaves

Tangy garlic shoots

Sit some **garlic bulbs or cloves** in water, and in just a few weeks they will grow **delicious shoots** that you can snip off and add to savoury dishes such as soups, stir-fries, salads and sandwiches.

YOU WILL NEED • garlic bulbs (preferably organic) • clear shot glasses or tealight holders • scissors or sharp knife

Quick growing guide

10 minutes to prepare

Place in a sunny area 14-22°C (57-72°F)

Replace the water every day or two

No need to feed

Harvest shoots when 20cm (8in) or taller

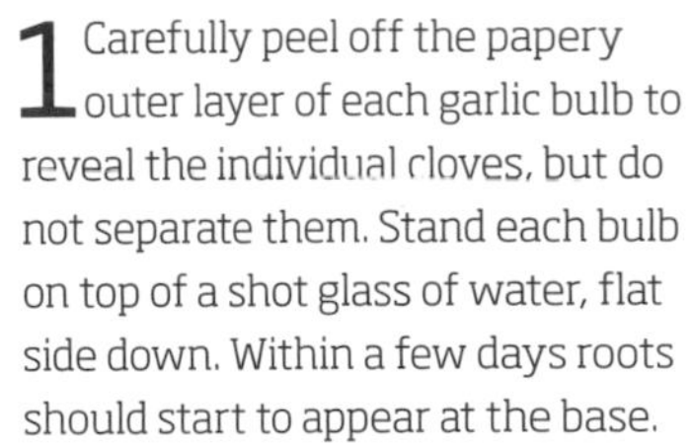

1 Carefully peel off the papery outer layer of each garlic bulb to reveal the individual cloves, but do not separate them. Stand each bulb on top of a shot glass of water, flat side down. Within a few days roots should start to appear at the base.

2 Keep the shot glasses and bulbs in a light area indoors, such as a kitchen windowsill or worktop. Replenish the water every day or two, and soon each garlic bulb will start to form a dense network of roots and green shoots.

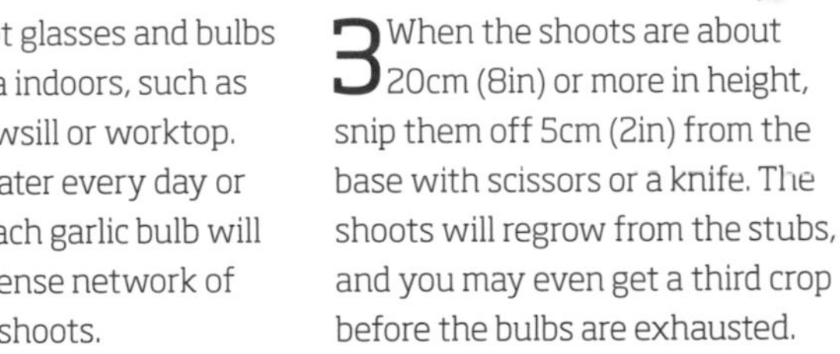

3 When the shoots are about 20cm (8in) or more in height, snip them off 5cm (2in) from the base with scissors or a knife. The shoots will regrow from the stubs, and you may even get a third crop before the bulbs are exhausted.

You can grow garlic shoots in shot glasses or little pots on any bright windowsill. Just ensure that the water is always topped up so the roots never dry out.
A second crop of sprouts will grow if you snip them off 5cm (2in) from the top of the garlic clove.

Chives & spring onions

Allium species

These diminutive plants are members of the onion family, and will produce crops from spring to autumn. You can use their mild-flavoured leaves and stems in many dishes.

How to grow

When to buy or sow

Spring onions are annuals, so buy new plants or sow seeds every year; chives are perennials and regrow each spring. Sow spring onion seeds in small pots using seed compost every few weeks from early spring to late summer for a continuous crop. If you buy spring onion seedlings, pot them up in multi-purpose compost. Sow chive seeds, or buy small pots of chives, in spring.

Light & heat

Both plants do well in pots on all windowsills except those that face north, which may not offer quite enough light. The plants are tolerant of cold conditions, and will also grow well in warm room temperatures.

Watering

Keep the compost moist, but don't allow it to become waterlogged. To prevent soggy compost, grow the plants in pots with drainage holes, and set these pots on saucers or inside waterproof containers.

Aftercare

Apply a liquid feed, such as diluted seaweed fertilizer, a couple of times during the plants' growing season to keep the leaves green.

Harvesting

Most spring onions are ready to harvest 6–8 weeks after sowing the seed. Chives can be harvested as soon as you have a large enough clump, but take just a few at a time so the plant can regenerate itself.

You can harvest and eat the chive flowers as well as the leaves.

Chives & spring onion 'Apache'

Choosing chive varieties

There are two main types of chive, and both produce leaves from spring to late autumn when grown indoors in pots. Keep the plants cool in summer to prevent them flopping, and water consistently.

GARDEN CHIVES ▶
(*Allium schoenoprasum*)
These slim-stemmed leaves have a mild onion flavour and produce edible pink pom-pom flowers in late spring.
Height: 30cm (12in)

GARLIC CHIVES ▶
(*Allium tuberosum*)
The thicker leaves of this plant, sometimes known as Chinese chives, have a stronger taste than the common garden variety, and combine garlic and onion flavours. They can be eaten raw or cooked.
Height: 50cm (20in)

Choosing spring onion varieties

Although there are a few varieties of spring onion, they differ very little in taste. Avoid types that produce large bulbs, as they may not develop well indoors. Spring onions may also be referred to in seed catalogues as "salad", "bunching", or "Welsh" onions.

◀ 'WHITE LISBON'
(*Allium cepa* 'White Lisbon')
A popular and reliable variety, with long white stems and dark green mild-flavoured leaves.
Height: 25cm (10in)

◀ 'PERFORMER'
(*Allium fistulosum* 'Performer')
This Welsh onion produces a bulb and has white stems with dark green leaves. It has a mild flavour that can be used to gently spice up salads and stir-fries.
Height: 30cm (12in)

'APACHE' ▶
(*Allium cepa* 'Apache')
An attractive purple-red stemmed spring onion with dark green leaves and a crisp texture. This variety is ideal for growing in containers.
Height : 25cm (10in)

Cooking with chives

Mash chopped chives into butter and use as a versatile accompaniment to steaks, fish, and vegetables.
Scatter chopped chives over braised spring onions and serve as a side dish.

Using spring onions

Chop spring onions, fresh tomatoes, ripe avocados, and jalapeno peppers, and sprinkle with grated cheese over a plate of nachos. Grill until the cheese melts.
Stir finely chopped spring onions and cucumber into natural yoghurt and cream cheese for an easy dip.
Embellish a simple miso soup with noodles and thinly sliced spring onions, raw carrots, and red peppers.

Miso soup with spring onions

Plant radishes and beetroot in pots with drainage holes set on trays or saucers. Place on a bench or tiled floor next to a large window or by a glass door.

Pots of tasty roots

Crunchy, peppery **radishes** are **quick to crop** and **easy to grow** indoors in a pot near a window. **Beetroot** take **longer to mature**, and you will need to take care of the plants for **a few months** to enjoy their sweet, nutritious roots (see project overleaf).

Choosing a container

To grow common round types of radish you can opt for a shallow container just 15cm (6in) in depth, but choose a slightly deeper pot if you are sowing 'French Breakfast' or the white mooli types. Beetroot requires a container at least 25cm (10in) deep and wide. Set the plants where they will receive lots of sunlight (north-facing windows will not be bright enough).

'French Breakfast' radishes in a wide galvanized pot

Root choices

There are many types of radish to choose from, but the easiest and quickest to grow are small round red types (see pp110–11 for other varieties). The best beetroot for indoor pots are also those that produce small round roots.

'Burpee's Golden' beetroot
With their orange skin and golden flesh, these beetroot look a little different; their golf-ball sized roots are also sweet and tasty.

'Cherry Belle' radish
The globe-shaped roots of this variety have a bright red skin encasing crisp white, mild-flavoured flesh.

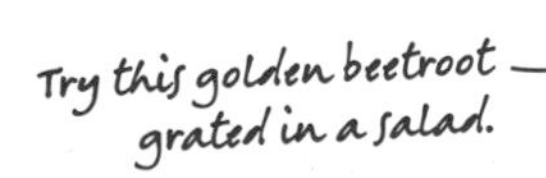

'Boltardy' beetroot
A popular beetroot that is slow to bolt (flower), this variety produces round roots with a superb sweet flavour and tender flesh.

'Barbietola di Chioggia' beetroot
This pretty variety of beetroot produces small round roots that feature concentric pink and white rings within.

Quick growing guide

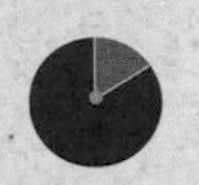

2-3 hours for various stages

Full sun

Water every 2 days

Feed beetroot with a fertilizer for leafy crops 6-8 weeks after planting

For radishes, harvest approx 4-6 weeks from sowing; for beetroot, approx 10-12 weeks after planting

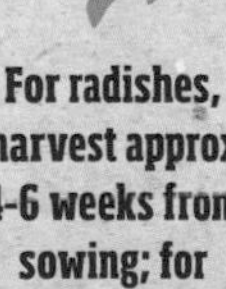

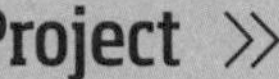

Grow **radishes & beetroot** in pots

These delicious roots will grow indoors from **spring** to **autumn**. They can either be raised from **seed** or from young **seedlings**, known as "plugs", which you can buy from the garden centre in spring. If you have space, **sow pots of radish seed every fortnight** for a continuous supply of fresh roots.

Water radishes consistently every couple of days to prevent the roots from cracking

YOU WILL NEED • 2 pots, one at least 15cm (6in) deep for radishes, and one at least 25cm (10in) deep and wide for beetroot • tray or saucer for each pot • radish seeds • beetroot plugs in cell trays • multi-purpose compost • watering can with rose head

Growing radishes from seed

1 Place the radish pot on its saucer or tray. Fill it up to 2cm (3/4in) from the rim with moist multi-purpose compost and firm it down gently with your hands. Use a blunt pencil to make two circular drills about 1cm (1/2in) deep on the surface. Pour the radish seeds into the palm of one hand and use your other fingers to sprinkle them thinly into the drills. Try to sow each seed about 5mm (1/4in) apart. Cover with compost and water gently, then place near a bright window.

2 Keep the seedlings well watered, but ensure the compost doesn't become wet. After 10-12 days, when the seedlings have a few sets of leaves, thin them out so the remaining young plants are about 2.5cm (1in) apart.

3 Water every two days, or every day in hot weather, and turn the pot often so the stems don't stretch towards the light and become long and thin. After 4-6 weeks, the roots will poke out above the compost. Pull the roots out gently by their leaves. Don't leave the radishes for too long in their pots once mature, as they can quickly become woody and inedible.

Growing beetroot from plugs

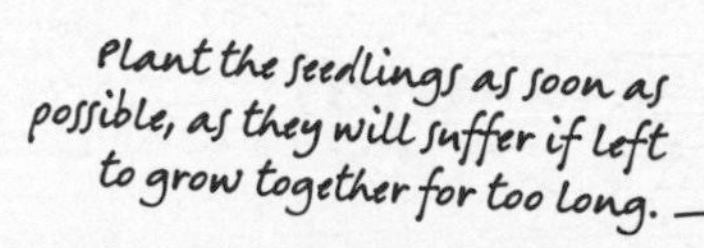

1 Fill the beetroot pot to about 2cm (¾in) from the rim with multi-purpose compost and firm it down gently with your hands. Water the seedlings well and remove one set from the cell tray.

2 Gently prize apart the individual seedlings from the clump, and try not to tear their delicate young root systems.

3 Make a hole in the compost with a blunt pencil and insert one seedling. Cover the roots with compost. Repeat with the other seedlings, 8cm (3in) apart.

4 Place the pot in a bright area. Keep the seedlings well watered, and turn the pot every week to ensure even growth. Harvest the beetroot when golf-ball sized and still tender.

Radishes

Raphanus sativus

The humble radish is a perfect crop for beginners to grow: it germinates quickly from seed, crops within a month of sowing, and is available in several jewel-like shades. Choose a few varieties to spice up your salads.

How to grow

When to buy or sow

Sow radish seed from early spring to summer in pots of multi-purpose compost. You can also buy young seedlings at a garden centre, but as the seeds germinate so quickly you may find it just as easy to sow them straight from seed. Long white mooli radishes can also be sown in autumn in a pot at least 20cm (8in) deep.

Light & heat

Radishes are cool season crops, and will struggle to germinate in temperatures above 21°C (70°F). If you want to sow them in summer, start them off in a cool room, or set the air-conditioning to 18°C (64°F). Mooli types need even colder conditions, so grow them in an outdoor windowbox in autumn if your home is too warm.

Watering

Regular watering is essential, especially during hot weather, and prevents the roots cracking and the plants running to seed.

Aftercare

Thin the seedlings when they are 5-8cm (2-3in) tall and have a few sets of leaves, to about 2.5cm (1in) apart. Do not feed the roots, as the compost contains sufficient nutrients.

Harvesting

Radishes are easy to harvest: simply pull out the plants individually by their leaf stems when you see their roots poking above the surface of the compost.

Plants need cool but bright conditions in order to thrive.

Best indoor varieties

You can grow a whole range of radish varieties at home, choosing from hot and spicy or mild types. Also look out for unusual colours such as black, white, yellow, and purple.

'SCARLET GLOBE' ▲
An award-winning variety that produces bright red, evenly shaped radish roots with crisp, tender flesh and a mild flavour.
Height & spread: 15 x 10cm (6 x 4in)

'ZLATA' ▶
An unusual yellow-skinned variety that produces oval-shaped roots with a peppery flavoured crisp white flesh.
Height & spread: 15 x 10cm (6 x 4in)

◀ 'SPARKLER'
These round, red-skinned roots have a white splash at one end. They are mild-flavoured and make a decorative addition to salads.
Height & spread: 15 x 10cm (6 x 4in)

'AMETHYST' ▶
The rich purple colouring of these roots makes a beautiful contrast with red radishes. They have a hot peppery flavour that packs a punch in salads and side dishes.
Height & spread: 15 x 10cm (6 x 4in)

◀ 'KULATA CERNA'
These unusual radishes have black skins and clear white flesh. The roots can grow up to 5–8cm (2–3in) in diameter without becoming woody, and retain their flavour when stored.
Height & spread: 15 x 15cm (6 x 6in)

'FRENCH BREAKFAST' ▲
A popular heritage variety, its cylindrical roots have a spicy flavour and a crisp, crunchy texture. 'French Breakfast 3' has white-tipped red roots.
Height & spread: 15 x 10cm (6 x 4in)

◀ MOOLI
Also known as daikon radish, the turnip-flavoured roots can be baked, boiled, shredded, or fried. They also store well. Sow from late summer to autumn.
Height & spread: 15 x 15cm (6 x 6in)

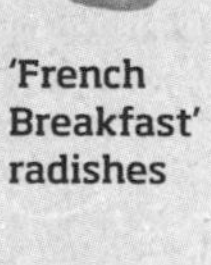

'French Breakfast' radishes

Cook's tips

Radish recipes

Thinly slice radishes and cover with salsa verde and shredded mint for a colourful starter.

Cut off and reserve the tops of some 'French Breakfast' radishes. Cut out the middle of each radish and fill with green or black olive tapenade. Replace the reserved lid and serve as an attractive appetizer.

Dip radishes in gently tempered butter, leave to set in the fridge, and serve with flaked sea salt.

Combine smoked salmon with chopped radishes and spring onions, add a yoghurt and horseradish dressing and serve as a starter.

Slice some radishes and add to a ham or cheese omelette just before serving.

Smoked salmon with radish

Level 2
moderate

Pots of **crunchy carrots**

Carrots can be grown **from seed** in pots indoors, and varieties are available **in a rainbow of colours**, as well as traditional orange (see project overleaf). The roots will grow best in a **cool** room with lots of **bright light**.

Carrots grown indoors are protected from carrot root fly, whose grubs eat the roots

Slow but steady growth

Growing carrots is not for the impatient gardener, as most varieties take at least eight weeks to mature from sown seed. However, by sowing a few pots in early spring, and more later on in summer, you can enjoy crops in summer and autumn. Grow carrots in a bright, cool room in a pot that allows for plenty of drainage (see project overleaf), as these vegetables will rot if left to sit in waterlogged compost.

Save small carrot "thinnings" to eat as microgreens

Choose seeds that produce a visually diverse crop

Colourful roots

Standard-sized orange carrots are widely available and not expensive to buy, so if you are growing them yourself, try a more unusual variety. Carrot seed is available for crops in a wide range of colours, including purple, yellow, red, and even white, or choose tiny round varieties, which will fit into shallow containers. You can grow the different coloured varieties in the same pot, but check the seed packets to ensure they need the same growing conditions and are about the same length, as this may affect the rate at which they mature. Galvanized buckets, colourful plastic bins, or wide deep pots, make good homes for a crop of carrots.

Create a display of carrot pots and herbs such as thyme, which will grow happily together in the same sunny situation. Keep the compost damp at all times, but ensure it never becomes waterlogged.

Grow carrots in pots

Growing carrots in a **plastic bin** with **drainage holes**, which is slipped inside a **waterproof container**, provides the **right growing conditions** for your crop while making a decorative feature for your home.

YOU WILL NEED • galvanized bucket or similar deep container • plastic bin to fit inside your container • hand drill with drill bit • multi-purpose compost & sieve • seed compost • watering can fitted with rose head • balanced liquid fertilizer

Open the windows whenever possible to provide your carrot crops with good ventilation

1 Choose a large watertight outer container that is at least 20cm (8in) deep for average-sized carrots, or 15cm (6in) for small, round types. Then find a plastic bin or similar lightweight pot to fit snugly inside the container. Turn the bin upside down and, using an electric drill, make five or so drainage holes in the base.

2 Fill the plastic bin with multi-purpose compost to about 8cm (3in) below the rim. You can also add a 1cm (½in) layer of seed compost on top, which will provide the optimum conditions for germination. Sow the carrot seeds thinly on top of the compost, and cover with 1cm (½in) of sieved seed compost. Firm the compost lightly with your fingers.

3 Place the plastic bin inside the waterproof outer container. Water the seeds gently with a watering can fitted with a fine rose head, or spray the surface of the compost well with a mister. Set the container in a cool room where it will get enough bright light. The seeds take a few weeks to germinate.

4 Keep the carrots well watered, but guard against soggy compost, as they dislike wet soil. If you overwater by mistake, remove the plastic bin and leave it to drain over a sink or in a shower, and tip out the excess water from the outer container.

5 When the carrots are between 10-12cm (4-5in) tall, thin any congested roots so that the remaining carrot seedlings are roughly 2.5cm (1in) apart. You can eat the tiny carrots you pull out raw and add their ferny leaves to salads and sandwiches.

6 The foliage will continue to grow as the roots develop. You will then see the tops of the roots starting to poke up above the compost. After 8-14 weeks (though some carrots will take longer) they will be ready to harvest.

Cool crops

Carrot seeds germinate best at a temperature of between 15-21°C (59-70°F) and the roots will grow well in a room no warmer than 20°C (68°F). When growing carrots next to a window, turn the container every day or two to prevent the leaves from becoming tall and leggy.

Feed your carrots every two weeks with a balanced liquid feed (unless you are using a compost already enriched with fertilizer - check the pack for details), and make sure the compost never dries out, especially during hot weather (see also step 4).

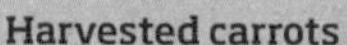

Harvested carrots

Carrots

Daucus carota subsp. sativus

These sweet roots are fun to grow indoors in large containers, and although this method will only deliver a small crop, the flavour of homegrown carrots makes them well worth the effort.

How to grow

When to buy or sow

Sow carrot seed from early spring to midsummer for a harvest through summer and autumn (see pp112–15). Raise the carrots in pots at least 20cm (8in) deep for average-sized carrots, or 15cm (6in) for shorter types.

Light & heat

Carrots germinate more quickly in warm conditions, so place your pots in a room at 21°C (70°F) and the seedlings should emerge within a week or two. They can then be moved to a slightly cooler, but bright, area to grow on.

Watering

Use a watering can with a fine rose head and water when the top of the compost feels dry; carrots will withstand some drought, but won't tolerate waterlogging.

Aftercare

When the seedlings are 10–12cm (4–5in) tall, thin them so those left are about 2.5cm (1in) apart. About four weeks later you can thin them further if you spot any that are still too congested. Feed weekly with an all-purpose fertilizer for root crops 6–8 weeks after sowing.

Harvesting

Harvest the roots while they are young and sweet – about 12–16 weeks after sowing. Check if they are ready by initially removing one carefully.

Some larger varieties of carrot may not grow as long in a pot, but are still full of flavour.

'Nantes' carrots

Best indoor varieties

There are hundreds of varieties of carrot available. You can either opt for reliable and smaller types, or be adventurous and try the more unusual purple and white forms.

'NANTES' ▶
This fast-maturing carrot produces blunt-tipped, almost coreless roots with a sweet crunchy taste. Sow in early spring or even late winter to harvest your first crops from late spring to early summer.
Root length: up to 15cm (6in)

◀ **'ST VALERY'**
This popular variety produces long, tapering carrots, which will be ready to harvest in late summer or early autumn. They take a few months to mature from a spring sowing, but your reward is sweet, crunchy roots.
Root length: up to 20cm (8in)

'WHITE SATIN' ▶
The vibrant white roots of this variety have a smooth texture and sweet flavour, similar to their more conventional cousins. These carrots retain their pale colour once cooked and make a pretty side dish when mixed with orange types. They are also delicious raw.
Root length: up to 20cm (8in)

'PURPLE HAZE' ▶
A beautiful colourful variety that is packed with antioxidants and vitamin A. Although this carrot loses its intense flavour and colour when cooked, the purple skin and bright orange flesh make an eye-catching dish when cut and served raw.
Root length: up to 25cm (10in)

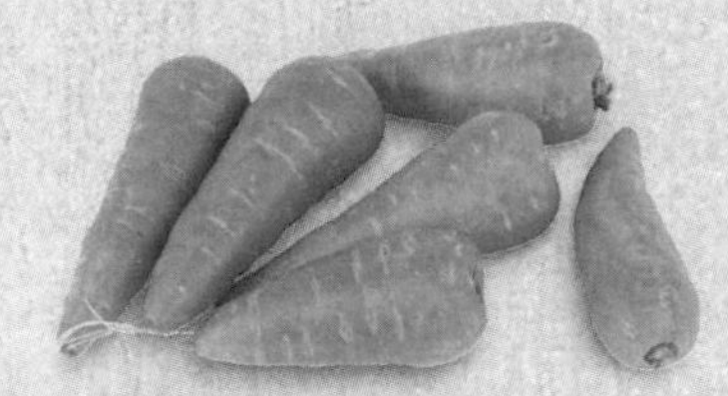

'ROYAL CHANTENAY' ▲
The squat, finger-length roots of this variety have almost no core and are perfect for growing in containers. Sow a few pots every 2–3 weeks from early spring to summer for a continuous harvest.
Root length: 10cm (4in)

Cooking with carrots

Slice raw carrots and serve with a hummus made from canned chickpeas, lemon juice, garlic, salt, cumin, tahini, and a little water blitzed in a food processor.

Substitute basil with carrot-top greens to make a mild-tasting pesto.

Mix coarsely grated purple and white carrots with currants, coriander, mint, and parsley, and top with crumbled feta for a visually dramatic salad.

Serve a striking canapé of thinly sliced raw purple carrots topped with crushed avocado, goat's cheese, and a roasted hazelnut on each.

Raw carrots with hummus

Quick growing guide

13 hours for various stages

Bright but not direct sunlight

Mist twice a day

No feeding required

Harvest within 2-3 weeks

Level 1 easy

Oyster mushrooms in 14 days

Watching fresh mushrooms grow **day by day** is fun and fascinating. You can choose to grow a wide variety of different types, including exotic **oyster mushrooms**, that are not readily available in the shops.

YOU WILL NEED

- oyster mushroom kit
- sharp knife
- large bucket or bowl
- clean brick or similar heavy object
- mister

Choose a kit with a "substrate" that has been pre-colonized with mushroom spawn. This kit uses spent coffee grounds (a waste product from the coffee industry) as its substrate

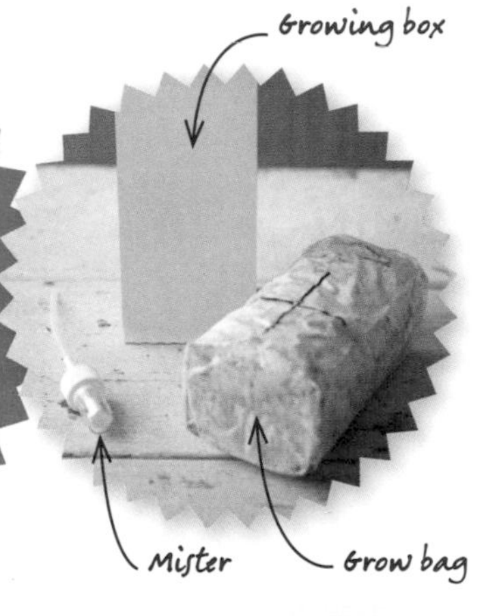

1 You can open a kit immediately or store it for up to a month in a dry, dark place. Remove the grow bag from the box and cut along the cross marked on the plastic.

2 Submerge the grow bag, cross side up, in a bowl of water and weigh it down with a clean brick or another bowl of water. Soak for 12 hours, then leave it to drain.

3 Squeeze out any excess water and air from the plastic bag, then slot it back into the box. Peel off the front of the box along the perforations to reveal a window.

The mushrooms are ready to harvest when their smooth caps start to turn up to reveal the serrated undersides. Repeat steps 1–4 for a second harvest.

4 Mist the open section of the bag with water twice a day until the mushrooms are ready to harvest. Nothing will happen for about a week, but you will then see tiny mushrooms starting to form. They will grow rapidly, often doubling in size day by day.

5 To harvest your mushrooms, gently grasp the whole bouquet at its base with one hand. Then twist and pull, and the mushrooms should simply break away from the bag, ready for use.

Mushrooms

Multiple species

You can grow a range of exotic and unusual mushrooms in your home, thanks to some ingenious kits that provide you with everything you need, including the spawn that develops into these tasty fungi.

How to grow

When to buy or sow

Most mushroom kits produce crops whatever the season. Some include a separate substrate (growing medium), known as fruiting cakes, which must be inoculated with mushroom spawn; others include pre-inoculated substrate and offer the best options for beginners. The substrate in a kit may be manure, sawdust, vermiculite, wood chips, or coffee grounds.

Light & heat

Mushrooms do not need light to grow – they are a separate category of living organisms – but most need a temperature of about 21°C (70°F) for the spawn to form the white mycelium from which the mushrooms develop.

Watering

Mushrooms need plenty of moisture to grow. Ensure the substrate and mycelium are always damp by spraying with water twice a day.

Aftercare

You can keep mushrooms in a bright room, but not in direct sunlight, as they will quickly dry out. Kits from specialist suppliers will specify the conditions required for their particular mushrooms.

Harvesting

To harvest your mushrooms, gently grasp the whole bouquet at the base. Then twist and pull, and the mushrooms should simply break away, ready for use.

Best indoor varieties

Some of the most unusual and beautiful mushrooms are the easiest to grow from a kit, while the button types – most widely available to buy in the supermarket – are among the most difficult. Check with specialist suppliers that the kits you intend to buy are suitable for growing mushrooms indoors.

SHIITAKE ▶
(*Lentinula edodes*)
Grown widely in the Far East, these mushrooms have a deep, meaty flavour when cooked. They are a vital ingredient in miso soup, stir-fry dishes, and a range of sauces.
Mushroom length: 5–10cm (2–4in)

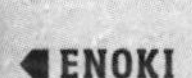

◀ ENOKI
(*Flammulina velutipes*)
These slim-stemmed, cream-coloured mushrooms have a mild, delicate flavour and a slightly crunchy texture. Eat raw or cooked in a range of dishes, including salads, sandwiches, soups, and pasta and noodle sauces.
Mushroom length: 15cm (6in)

KING OYSTER
(*Pleurotus eryngii*)
The cartoon-like appearance of this thick-stemmed, brown-capped variety belies its sweet gourmet flavour, which is very different from that of regular oyster mushrooms. Try sautéing, stir-frying, or grilling this regal mushroom.
Mushroom length: 15cm (6in)

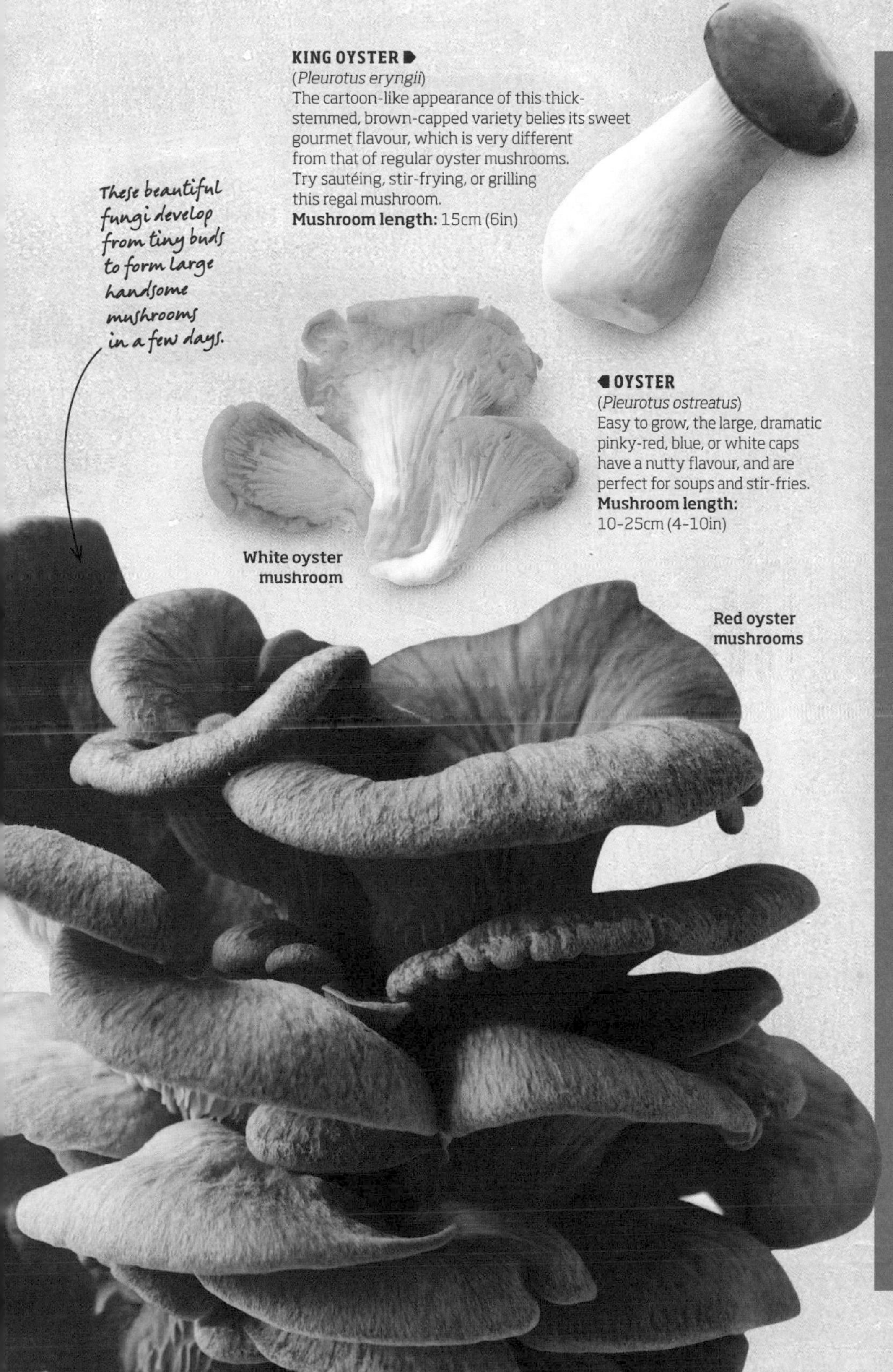

OYSTER
(*Pleurotus ostreatus*)
Easy to grow, the large, dramatic pinky-red, blue, or white caps have a nutty flavour, and are perfect for soups and stir-fries.
Mushroom length: 10–25cm (4–10in)

White oyster mushroom

Red oyster mushrooms

Cook's tips

Mushroom-inspired menus

Cut off and discard the lower half of a bouquet of enoki mushrooms and add the remaining caps and stems to a fresh salad.

Make garlic mushrooms by sautéing king oysters in butter and chopped garlic, then adding a handful of fresh chives on top before serving with garlic bread.

For a simple miso soup, add sliced shiitake mushrooms to a broth made from miso paste, sweet peppers, spring onions, and cubes of tofu.

Stir-fry some oyster mushrooms, spring onions, and pak choi, then flavour with sweet chilli and soy sauce before adding cooked soba noodles and serving.

Stir-fried oyster mushrooms

Fruiting vegetables

Tomatoes, aubergines, cucumbers, and peppers are all types of fruiting vegetable that can be grown indoors. They require a bright, sunny situation so if you have a light-filled room, try growing a few of these jewel-like crops.

Introducing fruiting vegetables

When is a vegetable not a vegetable? The answer is when it's a **"savoury" fruit**, such as a **tomato**, **cucumber**, or **pepper**, with its seeds wrapped in a nutritious fleshy case.

Sparkling show-stoppers

These wonderful fruit-vegetables are fun to grow, and while they take a little longer to mature than most leafy edibles they are beautiful plants in their own right and make decorative displays on windowsills and in sunny rooms. They are covered with pretty flowers in spring and summer, which then go on to form the fruits. They all require regular feeding, too, but by doing so you will ensure the heaviest crops. Check that you have space for larger plants such as cucumbers or a tamarillo tree tomato before you start growing them.

Healthy treats

Aside from the superior taste of homegrown crops, fresh fruiting vegetables are worth growing for their many health benefits. Tomatoes, for example, contain many minerals and vitamins, including A, C, and E. They are also rich in the natural "phytochemical" lycopene, which is responsible for their red colour; research has shown that this nutrient and antioxidant helps to support bone health and protects against diseases such as cancer. Cucumbers are a good source of vitamin K, which keeps the blood healthy, while peppers contain more vitamin C weight for weight than oranges. All fruiting vegetables are low in calories and contain fibre, and a diet rich in these foods will promote all-round good health and vitality.

Their versatility in the kitchen, and the fact that their vitamin and mineral content is greatest when they are eaten fresh, makes these vegetables a highly desirable addition to your indoor edible garden. All the plants included in this chapter require lots of sun for their fruits to ripen, so give them a go if your home receives plenty of natural light.

Best zones for fruiting vegetables

Like the majority of fruiting crops, these vegetables are sun-lovers and will thrive in the light and warmth of zones 1, 2 and 3. Cucamelons, chillies, sweet peppers, and bush, or patio, tomatoes will also grow well outside in summer.

South-facing windows
These plants relish the sun and heat beside a south-facing window. Try bush tomatoes, chillies, and peppers on a sill; set larger plants next to glazed doors or large windows.

East- and west-facing windows
Most fruiting vegetables will crop in a location close to a large east- or west-facing window, as long as the window is not shaded by trees or buildings.

Beneath a skylight
These plants will perform well under a skylight, especially if there is some supplementary sunlight pouring in from a vertical window. If the room is very hot, water plants daily.

Walls
Unless a wall receives full sunlight for most of the day in summer, the fruit on these plants may not develop well or ripen. Choose another location to be on the safe side.

Dark corners
You can only raise these plants in a dark corner if you have grow lights. Choose bush tomatoes, chillies, and peppers that will fit beneath a domestic grow light.

Centre of a room
Larger crops such as cordon tomatoes and cucumbers will grow well and fruit in the centre of a sun-filled, south-facing room, but not in any other location.

Cool (unheated) south-facing room
These crops will struggle in an unheated room in a cool climate in early spring. However, from late spring, the bright conditions will promote good fruit production.

Outside windowsill
All these plants are tender, which means they will die if temperatures plummet, so only plant outside once all risk of frost has passed in late spring or early summer.

Suspend the display from a secure hook in the ceiling. Choose a sunny spot for it to hang, and ensure you can reach it easily to water and feed the plants.

Chilli & herb **ball**

Suspended over a dining table, this hanging display of **chilli and bush basil plants**, with their jewel-like fruits and emerald leaves, is perfect for a home with **limited floor space** (see project overleaf).

Bowls as baskets

Metal or plastic mixing bowls make inexpensive and practical indoor planters, but you can use any lightweight watertight vessel as long as it is large and sturdy enough to accommodate your plants. Suspend the bowl using metal chains (used for traditional hanging baskets - see overleaf), or try jute macramé basket holders.

Chilli & herb choices

Some chilli plants grow tall and shrub-like so choose a dwarf or compact type for this project (below). Bush basil or thyme are the best choices of herbs, as both are compact and easy to grow.

Bush basil
Although it has smaller leaves than the common type of basil, bush plants are easier to care for.

Thyme
You can use thyme instead of basil; snip off the stem tips regularly to encourage new leaf growth.

Chilli 'Apache'
This variety produces fiery green chillies that turn red when ripe. Trim off stem tips while young to keep the plant small and productive.

Chilli 'Prairie Fire'
A compact variety, this plant will be smothered in hundreds of small, colourful, very hot chillies throughout the summer.

Quick growing guide

3-4 hours for various stages

Full sun

Water every 1-2 days

Feed weekly with high potash fertilizer when chilli flowers appear

Harvest when chillies are ripe; snip off basil leaves as required

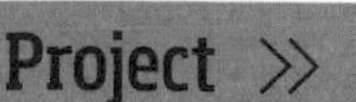
Project >>

Make a chilli & herb ball

Start this project in **late spring** or **early summer** when the chilli and herb plants are **young** and **small** enough to plant through the **holes in the basket**. If you accidentally damage any **leaves** or **stems** in the process, simply snip them off with a sharp pair of scissors and the plant should quickly recover.

Feed the plants weekly with tomato fertilizer when the chilli flowers appear

YOU WILL NEED

- metal hanging basket, coir liner, and basket clips
- small plastic bottle
- metal skewer
- sharp scissors
- approx 5 dwarf chilli plants and 5 bush basil plants
- kitchen cloth
- bowl or large jar for support
- multi-purpose compost enriched with fertilizer and mixed with vermiculite
- mixing bowl the same diameter as the hanging basket
- plastic bowl that fits inside the mixing bowl
- polystyrene pieces
- chopping board or scrap wood
- 10 short lengths of galvanized wire
- 3 galvanized chains approx 1m (3ft) depending on how low the ball will hang, and large curtain ring
- butcher's hook & sturdy ceiling hook

1 Cut the base off a small plastic water bottle that will fit through the holes in the basket. Keep the lid screwed on. Heat the end of a metal skewer, make a few holes in the sides of the plastic bottle, and insert it through a gap in the base of the upturned basket.

2 Using scissors, cut 10 evenly spaced large crosses in the coir liner, and a hole in its base for the bottle. Fit the liner inside the basket. Wrap the stems of a chilli plant in a kitchen cloth. Push the stems through a cross in the base, leaving the rootball inside.

3 Gently remove the kitchen cloth and set the basket, with the chilli plant hanging from its base, over a bowl or a large jar to support the basket without damaging the plant's stems. Then work your way around the basket, inserting more chilli and herb plants alternately in the same way.

4 Fill in around the rootballs of the plants with a mix of multi-purpose compost (enriched with fertilizer) and vermiculite. Fill right to the top of the basket, then press the soil down gently to ensure there are no air gaps.

5 Make 4–6 drainage holes in the base of the plastic bowl, then 8–10 more holes just below its rim, with the heated skewer. Half-fill the bowl with small polystyrene pieces and then the vermiculite and multi-purpose compost mix, firming it down well. Add a little more compost on top to make a slight mound.

6 Place a large chopping board or piece of scrap wood over the top of the basket and invert it. Sit the board on the bowl, then carefully slide it out so the basket sits directly on top of the bowl. Push the water bottle down into the soil if it protrudes.

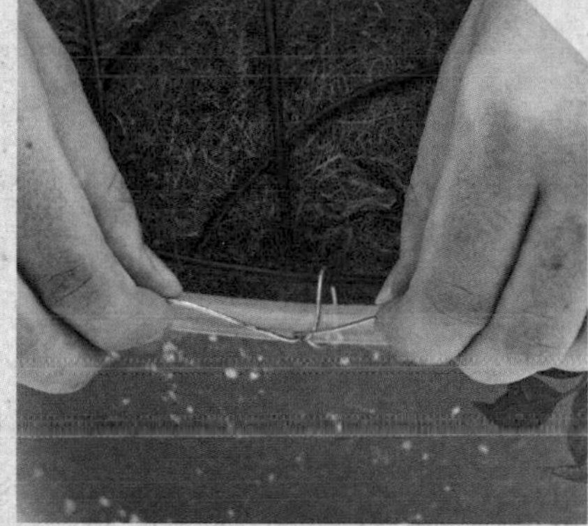

7 Thread one short length of wire through a hole below the bowl's rim. Bend the wire round so it loops over the rim of the basket to make a ring and bind the basket to the bowl. Secure the wire firmly. Repeat with the remaining holes.

Hang the basket below a skylight or close to a sunny window and turn it every week...

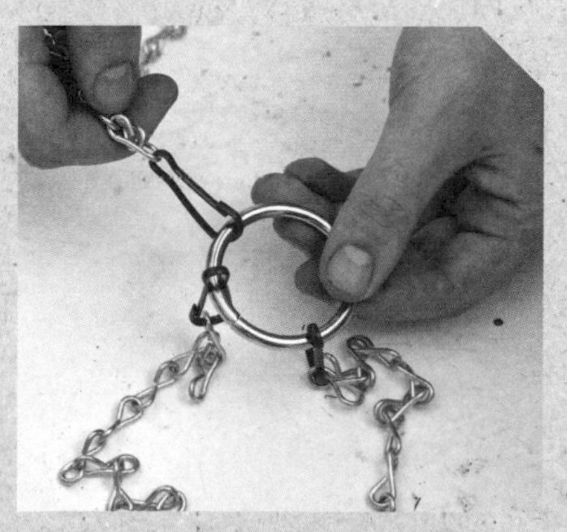

8 Fix a hanging basket clip onto one end of each galvanized chain, then clip it onto a curtain ring. Place the chilli and herb ball inside the metal mixing bowl and then sit it on the bowl or jar support.

9 Position the curtain ring at the base of the ball. Arrange the chains evenly around the sides of the ball and gather them together above it. Attach the chains to a butchers hook and hang from a hook fixed to a ceiling beam. Water the ball every day or so through the bottle in the basket.

Chilli peppers

Capsicum species

The bright fruits that adorn these pretty plants in late summer and autumn provide essential ingredients for a whole host of spicy dishes, from Indian curries to Asian stir-fries.

The small chilli fruits ripen from purple to red.

'Loco' chilli

Chilli heat ratings

Chillies contain capsaicin, a chemical which stimulates the nerve endings in the mouth that respond to heat. The strength of a chilli is measured by a scale known as Scoville Heat Units (SHU):

- Mild: up to 5,000 SHU
- Medium: 5,000 - 35,000 SHU
- Hot: 35,000 - 100,000 SHU
- Very hot: 100,000 - 500,000 SHU
- Sizzling: 500,000 SHU +

How to grow

When to buy or sow

As chillies have a very long growing period, sow the seeds in a heated propagator in late winter to guarantee fruiting crops; a grow light will help to ensure success. An easier option is to buy plants in spring, but the choice of varieties will be limited. Pot up the plants in multi-purpose compost.

Light & heat

Chilli seeds need heat to germinate – ideally 25–30°C (77–86°F) during the day and a warm room no lower than 15°C (59°F) at night. The hotter types, such as Habanero chillies, may take a few weeks to emerge, and all chilli plants demand full sun in order for the fruits to develop.

Watering

Water your chillies little and often so that the compost is moist at all times, but take care to avoid waterlogging the plants.

Aftercare

Keep the plants warm and pot on to increasingly larger containers as they grow. You may need to stake taller varieties. Feed weekly with a high potash fertilizer as soon as the flowers appear.

Harvesting

Cut off the chillies with sharp secateurs. Eat them fresh, freeze them whole, or string them up and air-dry them gradually in a warm room.

Best indoor varieties

There are a number of different chilli species, including the fiery Habanero types (*Capsicum chinense*), the equally hot Aji chillies (*Capsicum baccatum*), and those related to the sweet chilli, which range from mild to hot (*Capsicum annuum*). Wear plastic gloves and protect your eyes when preparing hot chillies.

'CAYENNE' ▶
(*Capsicum annuum* 'Cayenne')
A classic medium-to-hot chilli (30,000–50,000 SHU) with long, pencil-thick, wrinkled fruits that mature from green to red on tall plants. They can be eaten fresh or cooked.
Height & spread: 90 x 60cm (36 x 24in)

'JALAPENO' ▲
(*Capsicum annuum* 'Jalapeno')
Bullet-shaped and not too hot, these Mexican green chillies can be left to ripen to red. Ideal for pizzas and Mexican dishes, the fruits have a rating of 2,500–8,000 SHU.
Height & spread: 75 x 50cm (30 x 20in)

◀ **'DORSET NAGA'**
(*Capsicum chinense* 'Dorset Naga')
One of the hottest chilli peppers (just over a million SHU), this Habanero chilli produces pale green puckered rounded fruits that mature to red.
Height & spread: 75 x 50cm (30 x 20in)

'LOCO' ▲
(*Capsicum annuum* 'Loco')
This compact plant produces small oval-shaped purple fruits that ripen to red. It is ideal for growing on a sunny windowsill. The fruits have a moderately hot 24,000 SHU rating.
Height & spread: 30 x 40cm (12 x 16in)

'AJI AMARILLO' ▶
(*Capsicum baccatum* 'Aji Amarillo')
This Peruvian native produces green bullet-shaped fruits that turn orangey-yellow and have a smoky-fruity flavour. Produced on compact plants, the hot chillies have a Scoville rating of 30,000–50,000 SHU.
Height & spread: 60 x 50cm (24 x 20in)

◀ **'LEMON DROP'**
(*Capsicum baccatum* 'Lemon Drop')
A hot (30,000–50,000 SHU) lemon-flavoured chilli pepper, with small green slender fruits that ripen to yellow.
Height & spread: 60 x 50cm (24 x 20in)

'CHILLY CHILI' ▶
(*Capsicum annuum* 'Chilly Chili')
The small green fruits, which ripen to yellow, orange, then dark red, are mild with a 2,000–5,000 SHU rating, and perfect for those who like just a little heat.
Height & spread: 30 x 35cm (12 x 14in)

Turning up the heat

Stuff deseeded mild-to-hot chillies with a mix of soft cheese, grated Cheddar cheese, and chopped herbs. Drizzle with oil and grill until soft and lightly browned.

Finely chop tomatoes, deseeded chillies, onions, and fresh coriander, transfer to a bowl, add the juice of a lime and olive oil, and mix well for a spicy salsa.

Chilli & tomato salsa

Marinate deseeded large chillies in rum, then fill with a chocolate ganache and coat with melted dark chocolate for a fiery dessert.

Sauté whole chilli peppers until tender and golden, sprinkle with coarse sea salt, and serve as a tapas dish.

A galvanized tub is a great choice for large fruiting vegetables, providing plenty of space for plants and handles to make it easier to move around so your crops all receive sufficient light.

Ensure your container is watertight before adding any plants.

Mediterranean mix

Group a range of vegetable plants that enjoy the **same growing conditions** and **ripen** at more or less the same time to produce a large, **colourful display** of edible crops for your home (see project overleaf). You will need to care for the plants until the fruits are ready to harvest, but the results are well worth the effort.

Life in the sun

Not surprisingly, vegetables such as tomatoes, peppers, and aubergines - which are grown in abundance in Mediterranean regions and are essential ingredients in many of the local dishes - all need plenty of heat and sun to thrive. Choose an area in your home that is close to a large south-facing window or beneath a skylight, and a container that affords plenty of drainage, to provide the perfect growing conditions for this mix. If you don't have sufficient space for the whole group, you can simply grow one or two of these plants in large pots on a sunny windowsill - just follow the same growing tips described overleaf.

After the flowers appear, feed your plants weekly with a high potash fertilizer

Choosing your plants

There is a wealth of fruiting vegetable varieties you can choose for this display, but remember to check before buying that the plants you select will not outgrow your allocated space. You may also like to add a pot of chillies, as they require the same growing conditions.

Grafted aubergine plants are disease-resistant.

Aubergines

Most aubergine plants do not grow much taller than 75cm (30in), and will thrive indoors. Choose from white, purple, or striped varieties.

Cordon cherry tomatoes produce abundant crops.

Tomatoes

Small bush varieties of tomatoes - often used in hanging baskets - or compact cordon (also known as indeterminate) types will be perfect for this project.

Sweet peppers

Peppers come in a range of sizes, colours, and shapes, and you can even buy two types grafted onto one plant. Taller varieties may need staking as they grow.

Try growing some long Italian-type sweet peppers.

Quick growing guide

4-6 hours for the various stages

Full sun

Water every 2-3 days

High potash feed weekly

Harvest 12-16 weeks after planting

Project >>

Plant up a **Mediterranean mix**

The fruiting vegetables here have all been planted in **separate containers**, which have then been grouped inside a large galvanized tub. This technique ensures that each plant has **sufficient compost to thrive**, and individual plants can be removed once their fruits have been harvested.

Without insects to pollinate the flowers, you may need to do this job yourself (see p207)

YOU WILL NEED

- large container such as a galvanized tub, plus enough plastic (such as a large bin liner) to line the base if it isn't watertight
- small bag of gravel
- large bag of polystyrene pieces and polystyrene chips
- several plastic pots, about 20cm (8in) in diameter, for the plants
- multi-purpose compost
- enough tomato, aubergine, and pepper plants to pot up in the plastic pots inside the container
- decorative plant stakes, such as spiral supports, which come in a range of lengths, or bamboo stakes (one per pot)
- long length of soft twine
- watering can fitted with rose head
- secateurs or sharp scissors

1 If your tub is not waterproof, line it with plastic (such as a large bin liner), and add a layer of gravel on top to keep the plastic in place. Then include a layer of broken polystyrene pieces and chips on top of the gravel to create a reservoir area.

2 Set out the plastic pots inside the tub to determine how many plants will fit your display. Buy young tomato, aubergine and pepper plants; you need one for each pot. If growing from seeds, start them off about six weeks earlier (see pp204–05).

3 Fill one of the pots with multi-purpose compost up to about 5cm (2in) below the rim. Carefully plant an aubergine in the centre of the pot, adding more compost if needed. Firm the compost with your fingers to remove any air pockets.

4 Repeat step 3 with the other plants. Water them gently with a watering can fitted with a rose head. If growing grafted plants, ensure the graft (bump on lower stem) is above the compost.

5 Insert a stake to one side of each pot, carefully avoiding the plant rootball in the centre; decorative spiral supports look effective. As the plants grow, tie them to the stakes with twine.

6 Place the tub in a bright spot by a large sunny window or under a skylight. Turn it daily and swap the plants around occasionally so those in the centre are on the outside and all receive sufficient light.

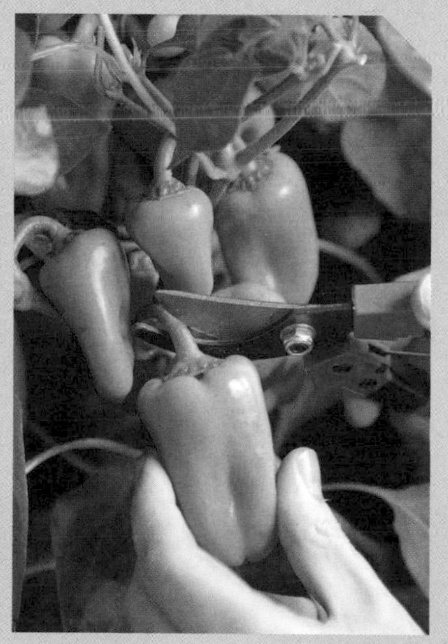

7 Once the flowers appear, feed plants with a high potash fertilizer every week. Open the windows frequently to increase ventilation. To harvest, cut off the ripe fruits with scissors or secateurs.

Pinch perfect

If you are growing cordon tomatoes, pinch out any shoots that grow between the main stem and side stems. This ensures that the plant puts its energy into making fruit rather than new green growth.

Pinch out any extra shoots

Aubergines

Solanum melongena

Delicious in Mediterranean dishes such as moussaka and ratatouille, aubergines come in a variety of colours and shapes, and the plants will grow successfully on a sunny windowsill.

Remove a few leaves if they are shading the ripening fruits.

These long, thin Asian aubergines are sweet and do not need salting before cooking.

Asian aubergine

How to grow

When to buy or sow

If you only have space for one or two – aubergines can grow up to 1m (3ft) tall – buy young plants in spring from a garden centre or online. If sowing from seed, start them off in late winter (see pp204–05 for sowing tips). Choose a deep pot at least 20cm (8in) in diameter, and plant one aubergine plant per pot. Use either a multi-purpose compost or a soil-based type compost, such as John Innes no 2.

Light & heat

Aubergines need plenty of direct sunlight in summer for the fruits to ripen, so position near a south- or west-facing window. The plants also require a minimum temperature of 16–18°C (61–64°F); higher daytime temperatures will help the fruits to ripen.

Watering

Water the plants regularly, but ensure the compost is never soggy; planting in a pot with drainage holes set on a saucer helps to prevent waterlogging. Mist the foliage every day with tepid water to discourage red spider mite and to help the fruits to set.

Aftercare

Apply a high potash liquid fertilizer every week or two once the first fruit has formed. With larger plants, remove any remaining flowers and cut off any unproductive side stems after five or six aubergine fruits have set. Stake plants when they are 20cm (8in) tall and tie in the stems regularly.

Best indoor varieties

The most widely available aubergines are dark purple and Zeppelin-shaped, but there is a much greater choice of sizes and colours available for more adventurous gardeners. You may only find a limited selection for sale as young plants, but seed companies offer a broad range of varieties.

THAI AUBERGINES
These golf-ball sized aubergines are white, green or striped, but are also available in red and purple. Often used in Thai curries, the fruits are crunchy and slightly bitter. Because they are small, you can leave several fruits on the plant to mature. **Size of fruit:** approx 2-5cm (3/4-2in)

'BLACK BEAUTY'
A popular variety, 'Black Beauty' produces large, glossy, dark purple fruits. The tall, sturdy plants yield six or more large fruits, which mature early and have soft, edible skins and seeds. Two plants will keep you in aubergines from summer until late autumn. **Size of fruit:** approx 10-15cm (4-6in)

'PINSTRIPE'
The oval, striped fruits appear from summer to autumn. Compact and sturdy, the plants are ideal for windowsills. Leave three or four aubergines on each plant if you want them to grow to full size. **Size of fruit:** approx 8-10cm (3-4in)

'RAJA'
Aubergines were originally white and looked like eggs, which is why they are known as eggplants in the US. This sturdy variety produces an early crop of small white fruits. Fruity and mild in flavour, these have tough skins, which should be removed prior to eating. **Size of fruit:** approx 8cm (3in)

Cooking aubergines

The easiest way to cook aubergine is to brush some slices with olive oil and bake them in a hot oven for 15 minutes or griddle them on a hot pan, turning them every so often until they are cooked through.

To make a simple vegetable ratatouille, heat a little oil in a large pan, and add some chopped aubergines, courgettes, sweet peppers, onions and garlic. Stir for 3 minutes until the vegetables are soft. Reduce the heat and add a can of tomatoes and a tablespoon or two of tomato paste. Simmer for 15 minutes, then stir in some fresh basil before serving.

Cut the stalk just above the aubergine's cap, or calyx

When to harvest

Aubergines have a long growing season, and if you buy a young plant it may take up to five months to produce mature fruits. Harvest the fruits from midsummer to autumn: cut them from the plant using a pair of sharp scissors or secateurs when they are glossy, plump, and a good size.

Storage & preserving
Most aubergines develop at slightly different rates, which means you will rarely have a glut and can enjoy them fresh, especially if you are growing just a few plants. You can store the fresh fruits for up to two weeks in the fridge, or you can cook and then freeze them.

For the fruits to ripen, set your aubergines in a warm room with plenty of direct sunlight

All parts of a tomato plant are poisonous except for the delicious, nutrient-packed fruits

Choose a large colander for your bush tomatoes. Leave it unpainted for a chic metallic look or apply a non-toxic metal paint. It also needs a plastic liner and pot to make it waterproof.

Tiny tomatoes in a colander

Bush tomatoes are the perfect crop for a **large colander**, which you can transform into a **hanging basket** (see project overleaf) or simply set on a table near a sunny window. The small sweet tomatoes tumbling from the plants in **late summer** will make a healthy snack or fresh salad ingredient.

Locating the right spot

Tomatoes are sun-loving crops and need a bright, sunny location to thrive in your home. An area under a skylight or close to a south-facing window will be most suitable. Turn the crops every day or two to ensure all sides of the plants and their developing fruits receive sufficient sunlight, and open the windows in warm weather to increase the air circulation around the plants. This promotes healthy growth and encourages the fruits to set.

Table-top display beneath a skylight

Choosing tomatoes

Look for bush tomato varieties, which have a cascading habit and, unlike the tall, upright varieties known as cordons, need no training or pinching out of side shoots. Good varieties include 'Balconi', 'Tumbling Tom', and 'Hundreds and Thousands'.

'Balconi'
Choose from the red or yellow variety of this compact, exceptionally sweet cherry tomato; its cascading habit suits a colander basket.

'Tumbling Tom'
This variety is one of the best choices for a hanging container, and forms a compact plant covered with a heavy crop of sweet, juicy red or yellow cherry tomatoes.

Choose a yellow- or red-fruited form of this reliable variety.

Quick growing guide

1-2 hours for various stages

Full sun

Water every 2 days

Feed with high potash fertilizer weekly when flowers appear

Harvest mid- to late summer

Project >>

Planting tomatoes in a colander

This large **colander hanging basket** is quick and easy to make and will provide a home for **three to four tomato plants**. You can also add an olla (ceramic jar) in the centre, which gradually releases moisture to the thirsty tomato plants, saving you the time and effort of watering them every day.

A smaller colander can be used for this project, with just one tomato planted in the centre

YOU WILL NEED • large colander • non-toxic metal paint (optional) • bubble plastic or heavy-duty bin liner • washing-up bowl or similar vessel to fit into the colander • screwdriver • multi-purpose compost • 3-4 bush tomato plants • watering can fitted with a rose head • olla (optional) • chains from a wire hanging basket • sturdy hook

1 Paint or spray the outside of the colander with a non-toxic metal paint, if required, and allow to dry thoroughly. Line the colander with a plastic material, such as bubble wrap or a heavy-duty bin liner, to make it watertight.

2 Buy or upcycle a plastic washing-up or mixing bowl that will fit snugly inside the plastic-lined colander and drill several drainage holes in the bottom of it with a screwdriver. Set the bowl inside the lined colander ready for planting.

3 Fill the bowl with multi-purpose compost to about 3cm (1¼in) below the rim. Water your tomato plants and gently remove one plant from its pot. Make a hole in the compost and plant the tomato, ensuring its rootball is completely covered.

4 Firm the compost around the rootball. Repeat the planting process with the remaining tomato plants, leaving a space of at least 15cm (6in) between each central stem. Water gently with a watering can fitted with a rose head to settle the compost around the roots.

5 Fill the olla with water and half bury it in the centre of the bowl. If hanging the colander, attach the chains by clipping them into some colander holes and hang from a sturdy hook fixed to the ceiling.

Caring for tomatoes

An olla (below) will continually release moisture into the soil, but check the compost every few days – especially if you have planted three or four tomato plants – and if it feels dry, add more water directly onto the compost. If you do not have an olla, water your tomato plants every day or two, but ensure the compost never becomes waterlogged. Erratic or irregular watering can cause the tomato fruits to split.

Most multi-purpose composts are enriched with fertilizers, which will feed the tomato plants until they flower, after which apply a weekly dose of high potash tomato fertilizer. Tomato plant flowers are self-pollinating and the fruits should set indoors, but by opening the windows to create a breeze or shaking the plants gently every two to three days, you will help to release the pollen that ensures the blooms will go on to produce tomatoes.

Water the compost if it feels dry

Tomatoes

Solanum lycopersicum

Nothing comes close to the taste of sweet, juicy homegrown tomatoes. Despite their exotic looks, they are deceptively easy to grow indoors as long as you have the bright, sunny conditions the fruits need to ripen.

If the leaves start to turn yellow, apply a magnesium feed to green them up again.

How to grow

When to buy or sow

Grow from seed from early spring (pp204–05), or buy young plants later in spring. Some plants reach up to 1m (3ft) or more in height; if space is tight, opt for a bush, or compact patio, variety. Grow in pots of multi-purpose compost. Except for patio tomatoes, each plant requires a pot at least 20cm (8in) in diameter and depth.

Light & heat

Tomatoes require plenty of sunlight – a shaded spot will result in few, if any, ripe fruits – and temperatures of between 21–24°C (70–75°F). The plants will perform poorly below 16°C (61°F) or above 27°C (81°F).

Watering

Water consistently and never allow the leaves to wilt, particularly after the fruits have formed, as this can lead to split fruits. Prevent waterlogged compost by planting in pots with lots of drainage.

Aftercare

Tie cordon plants to tall supports (p144) and remove any shoots between the main stem and side shoots (except on bush and patio varieties). Feed weekly with a tomato fertilizer when the flowers appear.

Harvesting

In summer and early autumn, when the fruits turn the right colour and size, cut off the long stems (trusses) with secateurs or a sharp knife.

◀ **'TOTEM' TOMATO**
Perfect for a windowsill, this F1 bush variety produces big crops of sweet medium-sized red fruits. **Height & spread:** 60 x 30cm (24 x 12in)

Choosing tomato varieties

Tomatoes come in many sizes, shapes, and colours, and there are both tall (cordon) and compact (bush or patio) types to suit your space, including the old-fashioned heritage tomatoes and sweet cherry varieties.

◀ 'TIGERELLA'
This cordon heritage variety produces high yields of medium-sized pretty red and yellow striped fruits. It grows very tall if planted in a large pot. **Height & spread:** up to 200 x 50cm (79 x 20in)

'SATYNA' ▲
A reliable beefsteak variety, which produces large meaty fruits – ideal for cooking or eating fresh. Stake well to prevent the stems snapping under the weight of the fruit. **Height & spread:** up to 200 x 50cm (79 x 20in)

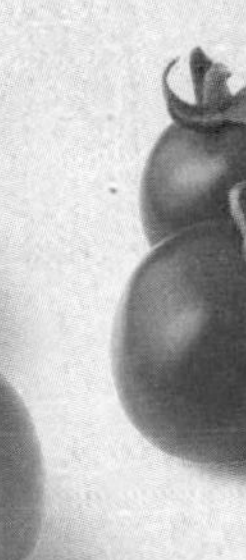

'BLACK CHERRY' ▶
The heavy crops of beautiful dark brown-red sweet cherry tomatoes produced by this heritage cordon variety make a real talking point.
Height & spread: up to 200 x 50cm (79 x 20in)

'VILMA' ▲
Specially bred for growing in containers, this compact bush variety produces a heavy crop of sweet and juicy cherry tomatoes over a long period.
Height & spread: 60cm (24in)

◀ 'SUNGOLD'
An outstanding cordon cherry tomato with golden-orange sweet and juicy, thin-skinned fruits.
Height & spread: up to 200 x 50cm (79 x 20in)

'OLIVADE' ▶
A cordon variety that produces medium-sized plum tomatoes. These are sweet enough to eat fresh, but are also ideal for adding to stews and sauces.
Height & spread: up to 180 x 50cm (71 x 20in)

'MONEYMAKER' ▲
This reliable tall cordon tomato produces bumper crops of smooth, medium-sized red fruits renowned for their exceptional flavour. **Height & spread:** up to 200 x 50cm (79 x 20in)

Essential ingredient

Mix halved tomatoes with sliced strawberries and peaches, dress with olive oil and balsamic vinegar, and top with shredded mint for a zingy fruit salad.
Make a light salad dressing blending the seeds of a juicy tomato with olive oil, vinegar, and seasoning.
Halve large tomatoes and sprinkle with a mixture of breadcrumbs, herbs, oil, and garlic. Bake until crunchy.
For a panade, cut the crusts from 16 slices of bread, cut each slice into 4, and place alternately with large sliced tomatoes, sliced onions, and fresh basil in a baking dish. Drizzle with vegetable stock, top with Parmesan cheese, bake in a medium oven for 45 minutes, and serve.

Panade with sliced tomatoes

Quick growing guide

2 hours for various stages

Full sun

Water every day or two

Feed weekly with high potash fertilizer when flowers appear

Harvest when tomatoes are ripe

Level 2 moderate

Tomato towers

Cordon tomatoes are **tall plants** that produce heavy **crops of sweet, juicy fruits**. If you have a skylight or large south-facing window, plant them in deep containers placed either side of a doorway or window to make **eye-catching sentries**.

YOU WILL NEED • 2 young cordon tomato plants • 2 plastic pots 20-25cm (8-10in) in diameter • multi-purpose compost • 2 tall watertight containers to accommodate the plastic pots • bricks to support the plastic pots • 2 decorative trellis supports • garden twine • watering can • high potash tomato fertilizer

1 Grow the plants from seed on a sunny windowsill, removing any extra shoots as they appear (see p135). Transplant them into 20-25cm (8-10in) pots when they reach about 45cm (18in).

2 Place a couple of bricks in the base of each tall container and set a potted tomato plant on top. Ensure the lowest leaves are above the rim of the large container.

Use bricks or polystyrene trays to raise up the tomato plants.

3 Insert a trellis support at the edge of each tomato pot, and tie in the main and side stems with soft twine as shown.

4 Place the tomato containers under a skylight or close to a large sunny window. Water every day or two, and feed weekly with a tomato fertilizer when the flowers appear.

Use tall decorative trellis supports for your tomatoes and tie the main and side stems carefully to them to ensure none snap under the weight of the fruits.

Tamarillo tree tomatoes

Solanum betaceum

How to grow

When to buy or sow

Young tamarillo plants are available to buy all year round, but to ensure the plants are healthy they are best purchased in spring as new leaf growth is emerging (the plants are deciduous). Tamarillos grow rapidly, so ensure you can accommodate a large spreading plant that grows up to 2m (7ft) in height and almost as wide. Pot up the shrub in a large container filled with soil-based compost such as John Innes no 2.

Light & heat

This sub-tropical plant will thrive in the warmth of a centrally heated home, especially one where winter night-time temperatures do not dip much below 15°C (59°F). It is heat-tolerant and fruits best by a window or under a skylight in full sun.

Watering

Water your tamarillo tree every day or two from spring to autumn, as it needs plenty of moisture to sustain its huge soft leaves. Plant in a deep pot with good drainage, as it will suffer if it sits in waterlogged compost.

Although the tamarillo is native to the Andes, most commercially grown trees are now cultivated in New Zealand

Tamarillo trees live for many years and need plenty of space and a bright, sunny location indoors to thrive.

The huge leaves, which can grow to the size of two dinner plates, resemble those of a rubber plant.

Aftercare

A balanced, all-purpose granular fertilizer should be added to the compost once a year in spring. Also apply three doses of specialist fruit tree fertilizer each summer at monthly intervals after the clusters of white flowers appear. Don't worry if some of the lower leaves turn yellow and fall off; this is a normal process and does not mean the plant is diseased.

Harvesting

Tamarillos may not produce fruits in their first year but, in the right conditions, most will crop in the second year. Harvest the fruits with sharp secateurs when they are a rich red or yellow colour and are firm to touch. Remove the skin and most or all of the seeds before eating.

Flowers & fruit
The self-pollinating white flowers appear in spring, and later develop into the fruits. You can shake the tree gently or mist the flowers with water every few days to encourage the fruits to set.

Sharp fruits
Red- or pink-fruited varieties have a slightly sharper taste than yellow forms, and are delicious in salads.

Pruning a tamarillo

Once your plant reaches 1m (3ft) tall, cut off the top stem tip. This will encourage it to branch out, and prevent it from growing too tall. As the plant matures, prune the branches to create an open framework, and remove those branches growing from the base of the main stem. The fruit is produced on new growth, so each year in early spring cut back all the old stems that produced fruit the previous year.

Sprinkle halved tamarillos with sugar, pour over some red wine, roast until soft, and serve with Greek-style yoghurt.
Peel and dice blanched tamarillos, mix with chopped green chilli, diced onion, and coriander, and stir in a teaspoon of maple syrup and some olive oil for a salsa to serve with corn chips.
Try peeled tamarillo slices as a sweet and tangy alternative to tomatoes in green salads.
Top your toast with slices of tamarillo sprinkled with salt.
Replace tomatoes with tamarillos in a salsa recipe and serve with tortillas stuffed with beans, rice, and cheese.

Tamarillo salsa with filled tortillas

The cucumbers in this unit are growing in plastic pots with drainage holes, which are set inside waterproof containers to create the perfect environment for the thirsty cucumber plants.

Cucumbers on wheels

You can make a beautiful leafy **fruiting screen** in your home with a few **cucumber plants**, which will grow well and produce an abundance of tasty fruits in a **bright, sunny location** (see project overleaf).

Harvesting your cucumbers regularly encourages the plants to produce more flowers and fruits

Quick growing guide

4-5 hours for various stages

Full sun

Water every 2 days

Feed fortnightly when flowers appear with high potash fertilizer

Harvest about 12-14 weeks after sowing

Bring in the light

Cucumbers require plenty of light for the fruits to ripen, so you will need a large south-facing window and/or skylight for the plants to succeed. It's best to select a greenhouse variety of cucumber, and opt for an all-female type. This will mean that every flower will produce a fruit. Outdoor varieties can be grown indoors, too, but they produce non-fruiting male flowers that are needed to pollinate their female flowers (see p155).

Cucumber flower

Big & beautiful

Homegrown cucumbers tend to be more flavoursome than shop-bought varieties and are well worth a try if you have the right growing conditions. Before choosing to grow cucumbers indoors, ensure that you will be able to accommodate the large climbing plants, which can reach up to 1.5 metres (5 ft) in height and spread - although raising them in bespoke units (see overleaf) will help keep them in check.

Developing fruits
As each flower starts to fade, you will notice a baby cucumber growing just behind it. The fruits will then take a few more weeks to mature.

Young & sweet
Harvest your cucumbers with a sharp knife when they reach approximately the length indicated on the seed pack or plant label (if you bought seedlings).

Project >>

Make a cucumber unit on wheels

This **bespoke container on wheels** with a string support is ideal for **growing cucumbers indoors,** as it allows you to move them around so that all sides receive sunlight, and you can store the unit out of the way at night.

YOU WILL NEED

- large sturdy vegetable crate
- plywood, 18mm (3/4in) thick, cut to fit the bottom of the crate
- pencil
- tape measure
- hand saw
- electric screwdriver
- 20 x 20mm (1in) countersunk screws
- 4 x 25mm x 20mm (1 1/4 x 1in) treated wooden battens for the frame, cut to length (see steps 3-5)
- 8 x 25mm (1 1/4in) countersunk screws for fixing battens to crate in steps 4 and 5
- 4 non-marking swivel castor wheels
- thick garden twine

1 Place the crate on the plywood and draw around it with a pencil. Set the plywood on the edge of an old table – use a clamp if you have one to hold the wood – and cut along the markings with a hand saw.

2 Using 20mm (1in) countersunk screws and an electric screwdriver, fix the plywood piece onto the base of the crate at each of the four corners, making a small pilot hole first to prevent the wood splitting.

3 Cut four wooden battens to make a frame about 1m (3ft) tall and the width of your crate. Drill holes on the wide edge of each one at 10cm (4in) intervals; the first hole should be 10cm (4in) from one end.

4 Fix the two battens that will form the vertical sides of the frame at the back of the unit to the side edges of the crate, using two 25mm (1 1/4in) countersunk screws for each batten, one above the other.

5 To complete the frame, measure and trim one batten to fit between the uprights and another, slightly longer one, to fit on top of the uprights. Screw in place with 25mm (1 1/4in) countersunk screws.

6 Turn the unit on its side and fix a wheel at each corner using 20mm (1in) countersunk screws. The thread size of the screws depends on the wheel plate's holes.

7 Starting at the bottom left hole, thread the twine up, over, and down through all the holes in the horizontal battens, then through the holes in the vertical battens.

To make your cucumber unit stronger and more rigid, fix a zinc-plated steel angle plate to the top and bottom corners of the wooden frame, as shown

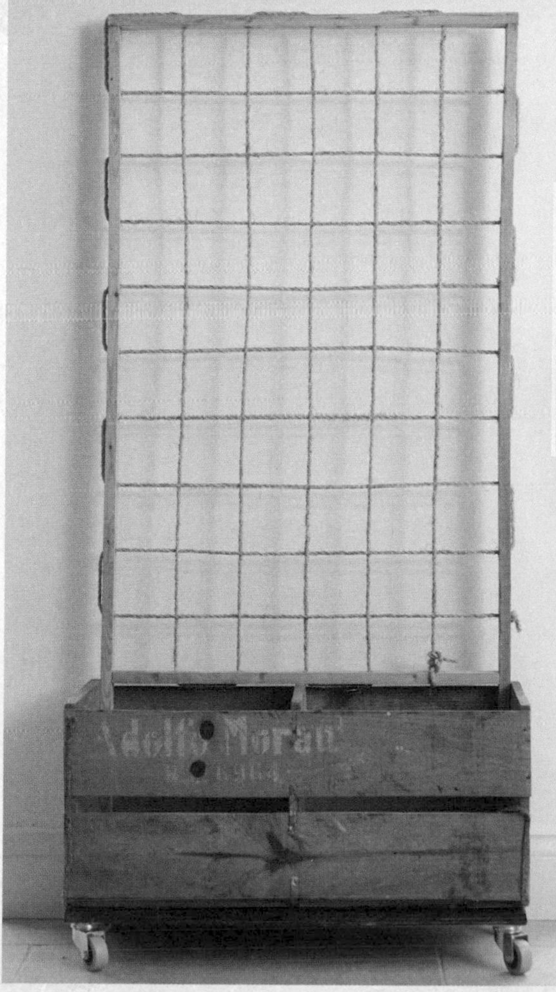

Tie a knot in the end of the twine before you start threading it.

Secure the twine lattice in place with another firm knot.

8 Pull the twine tight so that all the strings are taut. Then secure firmly at the end with a knot and cut off any excess string. The unit is now ready to plant up (see overleaf).

Easy trellis option

Instead of threading twine through a frame, opt for a quicker method and fix a ready-made wooden trellis in place. Follow steps 1-4, then screw the trellis onto the upright battens using 25mm (1¼in) countersunk screws. You can also paint the trellis and battens to match your decor.

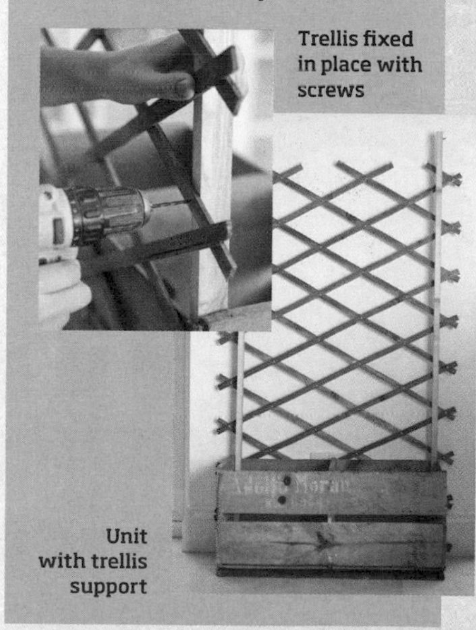

Trellis fixed in place with screws

Unit with trellis support

Project continues >>

Grow cucumbers for a crate on wheels

You can grow **cucumbers from seed**, or buy some young plants from a garden centre, and transplant them into the unit to create an **impressive display** of leaves, flowers, and full-flavoured fruits.

Cucumbers will thrive in a warm, bright room at a temperature of between 21-24°C (70-75°F)

YOU WILL NEED • small coir or plastic pots • cucumber seeds • seed compost • multi-purpose compost • watering can • 2 large plastic pots with drainage holes, plus 2 large plastic pots without drainage holes that fit inside the crate • garden twine • secateurs

1 Fill small coir or plastic pots with seed compost. Sow 2-3 seeds per pot and cover with 1cm (½in) of compost. Water well and set the pots on a tray in a warm, bright area such as on a windowsill. The seedlings should emerge within a week or two. When they have 2-3 sets of "true" leaves (rather than seed leaves), transfer each young plant into its own pot filled with multi-purpose compost (pp200-01) and grow on until 20cm (8in) in height.

Ensure the plastic pot with drainage holes fits easily inside the waterproof container.

2 Set two waterproof containers in the cucumber crate and slip plastic pots with drainage holes inside them. Fill these pots with multi-purpose compost to about 3cm (1¼ in) below the rim.

3 Transplant one or two young plants into each pot, firming them in gently to remove any air pockets. If you added a small stake to support the young stems as they grew, transplant that too. Water well.

4 Place the cucumber unit in a bright sunny location in your home; cucumbers will not flower and fruit well in low light conditions. As the plants grow, gently tie the stems to the twine lattice with some garden twine so the plants' leafy stems cover the support evenly.

5 Turn the unit every few days so the plants receive adequate light front and back. As soon as flowers start to form, feed the plants with a high potash fertilizer every two weeks. If you are growing a female-only variety, remove any male flowers if they appear (p155).

6 Remove any large leaves that shade the developing fruits and continue to water the plants well, ensuring they don't become waterlogged. Harvest the fruits with a sharp knife when they reach the length indicated on the seed pack or label.

Growing tips

For a good crop of cucumbers, pinch out the growing tip of the main stem as it reaches the top of the support. This encourages the plant to produce more side shoots. Look out for flowering side shoots and shorten these stems so that each has just two leaves beyond a female flower, which will have a tiny fruit growing behind it. Also pinch out the tips of non-flowering side shoots once they have grown to about 60cm (24in) in length.

Main cucumber stem

Cucumbers

Cucumis sativus

Sweet and juicy, the flavour and crisp texture of homegrown cucumbers is far superior to most shop-bought types. The large leafy climbing plants also make a decorative feature.

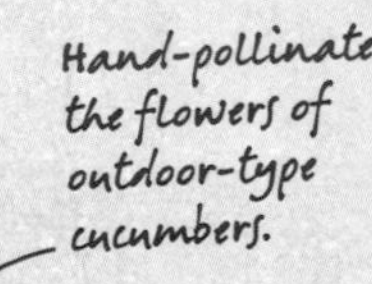

How to grow

When to buy or sow

Sow from seed in spring (see p152 for details) or buy young plants from a garden centre and pot each one individually into a large container of multi-purpose compost. When planting, insert a trellis or similar support at the edge of the container for the plant to climb up.

Light & heat

Cucumber seeds require a minimum temperature of 20°C (68°F) to germinate. Greenhouse cucumbers can be grown on in a warm room with a minimum night-time temperature of 15°C (59°F), but outdoor types will survive at lower temperatures. Set your cucumber plants in a bright sunny spot by a large window.

Watering

These thirsty plants require consistently moist, but not wet, compost. Plant them in pots with drainage holes and set the potted plants on saucers or inside waterproof containers. Mist the plants a few times a week to create the humid atmosphere they enjoy.

Aftercare

Take out the uppermost stem tip when each plant reaches the top of its support. Feed with a high potash fertilizer once a fortnight when the flowers appear. The flowers of outdoor cucumbers also need to be hand-pollinated every day or two – see p207 for details.

Harvesting

Cut the fruits off with sharp secateurs when they are firm to the touch and the size indicated on the seed pack or plant label. Fresh cucumbers will keep for a week to 10 days in the fridge.

Best varieties

There are two main groups: indoor greenhouse types, and smaller outdoor "ridge" varieties. Both can be grown indoors, but the outdoor types need to be hand-pollinated, and should not be grown near indoor cucumbers: if the male flowers (those without a tiny fruit behind them) of outdoor varieties pollinate indoor cucumbers, they make the latter's fruits taste bitter. Many greenhouse types are "all-female", producing only fruit-bearing female flowers that don't need pollinating, but they may produce male flowers, which must be removed.

'CUCINO'
The diminutive cucumbers of this greenhouse variety can be eaten without having to be peeled. The fruits are crisp and have a sweet juicy flavour. This is an all-female variety, so remove any male flowers if they appear.
Height & spread:
300 x 45cm (118 x 18in)

'DELIZIA'
This disease-resistant greenhouse type produces slightly ribbed small fruits with thin, almost translucent skins that do not require peeling. Remove any male flowers if they appear.
Height & spread:
300 x 45cm (118 x 18in)

'CARMEN'
Very disease resistant, this all-female greenhouse variety produces an abundance of dark green-skinned fruits with a crunchy texture. Remove any male flowers as soon as you see them.
Height & spread:
300 x 45cm (118 x 18in)

'BUSH CHAMPION'
An outdoor, compact variety that produces heavy crops of large, crisp, bright green cucumbers. Ideal for a small space, these plants can be trained up bamboo canes in a pot. Hand-pollinate the flowers (p207) to guarantee a good crop.
Height & spread:
60 x 20cm (24 x 8in)

'Bush Champion'

Cucumber delights

Make a quick *salade niçoise* of sliced cucumber, lettuce, ripe tomatoes, steamed whole green beans, boiled eggs, and tuna flakes.
Deseed and finely chop a cucumber and fresh mint. Mix with crushed garlic and Greek-style yoghurt to make a tzatziki-style dip.
Combine sliced cucumber, some sun-dried tomatoes, fresh basil, and halved falafels in a wrap for a healthy lunchtime snack.
Slice a cucumber and a bulb of fennel. Add them to a salad containing some mixed lettuce leaves, sliced celery, and chopped spring onions, and serve as a refreshing side dish.

Cucumber & fennel salad

The cucamelon's ivy-like foliage and striped baby fruits make a striking feature trailing from a wooden crate suspended beneath a skylight.

Cucamelons in hanging crates

Pretty **cucamelon fruits**, which hang like little green striped baubles from long trailing stems, taste like **cucumber** with a hint of **lime.** These sun-loving plants are perfect for growing in an indoor hanging basket or **wooden crate** (see project overleaf).

Cucamelons do not need peeling and make a great snack for a child's lunchbox

Refreshing fruits

You can buy young plants from online nurseries, but they are very easy to grow from seeds that cost a fraction of the price. Sow in pots in early spring and you will have a crop of juicy fruits through the summer. Try the fruits, which look like baby watermelons and are also known as mouse melons, sliced and mixed into salads, salsas, and vegetable side dishes, or eat them whole as a healthy snack.

Cucamelon fruits

Flowing stems

Cucamelon plants are vines and, as such, produce long stems and curly tendrils that cling to supports to help them climb. You can either allow the stems to trail over the sides of a hanging basket or crate, as shown here, or plant them in a large pot with a trellis fixed to the back and leave them to scramble up, like a baby cucumber. These native Mexican plants require plenty of sunlight, and are best grown near a south-facing window or under a skylight.

The plant's trailing stems can grow up to 1.2m (4ft) in length.

Cucamelons hanging by a sunny window

Quick growing guide

3-4 hours for various stages

Full sun

Water every 2-3 days

Feed weekly with high potash fertilizer when flowers appear

Harvest when fruits are grape-sized and firm

Project >>

Grow cucamelons in hanging crates

Raise these tiny fruity treasures **from seed** and make a home for them in a lined wooden crate suspended from the ceiling. Growing the plants in this way makes the fruits **easy to harvest** when they are the size of large grapes.

YOU WILL NEED

- 8cm (3in) plastic pots
- cucamelon seeds
- seed compost
- vermiculite
- wooden crate
- rope or thick twine
- large plastic pots to fit into crate
- multi-purpose compost
- waterproof sail cloth (or a heavy-duty black plastic bag) and a bulldog clip
- polystyrene pieces
- sphagnum moss (optional)
- large hook for ceiling
- watering can with rose head
- scissors

Cucamelon flowers must be hand-pollinated to produce fruits - see p207 for instructions

1 Fill a few small pots with seed compost. Sow 2-3 cucamelon seeds in each pot, and cover with a layer of vermiculite. Water and set on a sunny windowsill. The seeds may take a few weeks to germinate.

2 When the seedlings are about 8cm (3in) tall and have a few sets of leaves, transplant each into a small plastic pot of its own. To do this, hold the seedling gently by a leaf, remove the rootball with a spoon or fork, and transfer to the pot.

Plant the seedlings up into larger pots of multi-purpose compost.

3 Keep the seedlings well watered. A few weeks after transplanting them, buy two large plastic pots that will fit snugly inside your wooden crate. Pot up two young cucamelon plants into each large pot, and water them well.

Take care not to damage the stems when placing the pots inside the crate.

4 Line the crate with sail fabric or heavy-duty black plastic. Push it into all four corners, then fold over the top and tuck it inside the crate rim. Use a clip to keep the fabric in place while you do this.

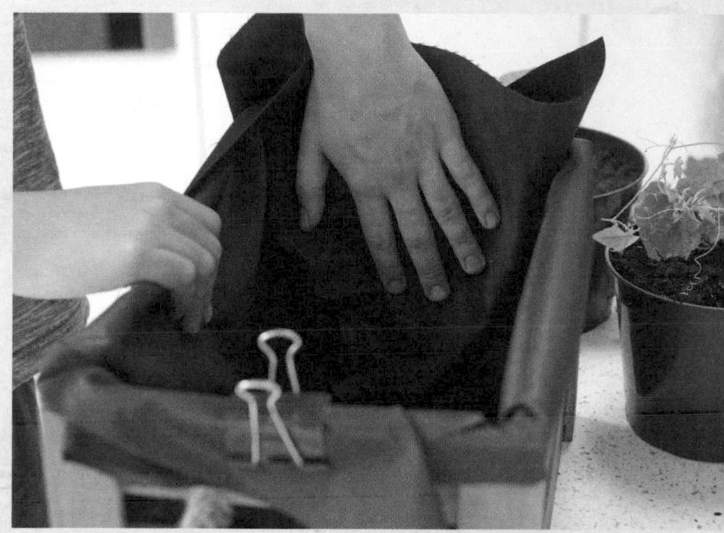

5 Set the two large pots of cucamelons inside the crate. If required, add some polystyrene pieces to the bottom of the crate to raise up the pots to the right level so they sit just below the rim.

Growing tips

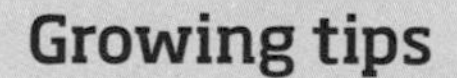

Water cucamelon plants every two to three days, but ensure the crates do not fill up with water. Turn the crate around every week or two, if suspended by a window, for even growth. Feed weekly with a high potash fertilizer, such as tomato feed, when the flowers appear, then pollinate the flowers by hand.

Water the plants regularly

6 Cover the pots with moss to help retain moisture. Hang the crate from a hook fixed into a cross beam in the ceiling with securely tied rope. Cut off all straggly stems just below a leaf to encourage more stems to form.

Raise **sweet peppers** in colourful pots

These handsome **exotic plants**, which hail from **Mexico** and **South America**, produce many colourful fruits from **mid-** to **late summer** or **early autumn** if you keep them in a sunny, warm room and feed them regularly.

YOU WILL NEED • plastic or ceramic pot at least 30cm (12in) in diameter and depth • drip tray • multi-purpose compost enriched with fertilizer • 3 sweet pepper plants (such as 'Luteus') • 3-4 creeping thyme plants (*Thymus serpyllum*) • watering can fitted with a rose head • 3 stakes • soft twine or plastic-coated plant ties • mister

Quick growing guide

1-2 hours for various stages

Full sun

Water every 2 days

Feed weekly with high potash fertilizer when flowers appear

Harvest when the peppers are fully formed and the right colour

1 Place the plastic pot on a drip tray if it has drainage holes, or choose a container with an integral watering system (p28). Fill to 5cm (2in) below the rim with multi-purpose compost. Plant the three pepper plants, spacing them evenly.

When the flowers appear, mist them every day or two to encourage them to develop into fruits

2 Add the thyme plants around the edge of the pot between the peppers. Firm the compost around the roots of all the plants to eliminate any air gaps. Water the plants, and add more compost if their roots become exposed.

3 Insert wooden stakes next to the inside edge of the rootball of each pepper plant. Using soft twine or plastic-coated plant ties, fix the main stem of each plant carefully to a stake. Continue to tie in the stems as the plants grow.

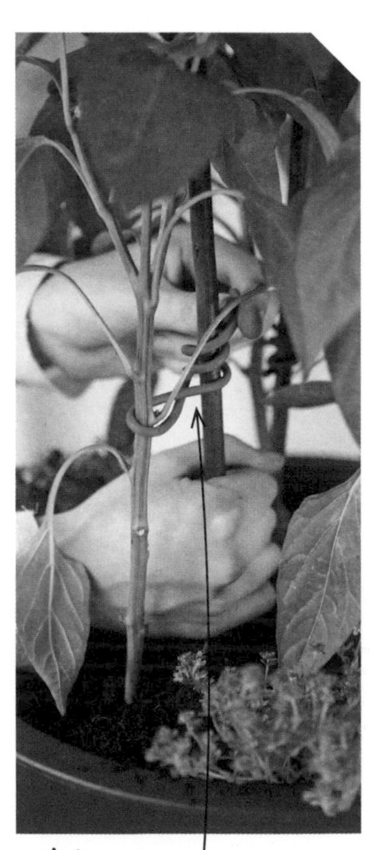

Tie the twine in a figure of eight.

When ripe, harvest the peppers by cutting them off close to the stem with sharp secateurs

Set your pot of peppers close to a south-facing window or directly below a bright skylight in a warm room to mimic the plants' native growing conditions.

Sweet peppers

Capsicum annuum

These vibrant fruiting vegetables are packed with antioxidants and vitamins, and are at their sweetest and crispest when picked straight from the plant. Eat raw or use to inject colour into baked Mediterranean dishes or Asian-inspired stir-fries.

How to grow

When to buy or sow

Sow the seed in early spring (see pp204–05) in pots of seed compost, or buy young plants from a garden centre later in the season. Repot into progressively larger containers of multi-purpose compost as they grow.

Light & heat

These Mexican natives like warm conditions; the seed will need a temperature of between 18–25°C (64–77°F) to germinate. The plants will grow on happily in a warm, sun-filled room close to a window or below a skylight.

Watering

Ensure you water every day or two, especially during hot weather. Avoid waterlogged compost by using pots with good drainage.

Aftercare

Stake tall plants (p160). When flowers appear, feed weekly with a high potash fertilizer. Mist the flowers every few days to encourage the fruits to set, and open the windows to increase ventilation whenever possible.

Harvesting

Ripe peppers are firm to the touch and approximately the size indicated on the plant label or seed pack. Remove regularly with secateurs to encourage more fruits to form.

Best indoor varieties

Sweet peppers come in a range of colours, although most green types will eventually ripen to yellow, orange, or red, and will sweeten as they mature.

'MOHAWK' ▶
These compact semi-trailing plants are perfect for pots on a sunny windowsill and produce heavy crops of small, block-shaped sweet peppers that mature to bright orange.
Height & spread:
50 x 40cm (20 x 16in)

'LUNCHBOX MIX' ▲
The small fruits produced by this medium-sized plant start off green and change to a mix of yellow, red and orange. The small sweet peppers are ideal for a lunchbox.
Height & spread:
90 x 45cm (36 x 18in)

◀ **'THOR'**
Tall and elegant, this plant produces long red peppers which have a sweet flavour and crisp texture. Ideal for slicing into salads, or for grilling or barbecuing.
Height & spread:
up to 150 x 60cm (59 x 24in)

'TEQUILA' ▲
The dark purple skins and white flesh of these medium-sized peppers make a dramatic contrast with red or yellow types. The fruits eventually mature to red.
Height & spread:
90 x 45cm (36 x 18in)

◀ **'LUTEUS'**
These bright yellow sweet fruits, which mature from green, are produced on a compact plant that is ideal for growing in a pot on a windowsill or sunny kitchen counter.
Height & spread:
60 x 40cm (24 x 16in)

◀ **'BONETA'**
This mini-fruiting pepper has lush dark green foliage and is covered with small pale green fruits that ripen to bright red in late summer.
Height & spread:
50 x 40cm (20 x 16in)*

Sweet pepper dishes

Grill some halved, deseeded red peppers, broccoli florets, and sliced red onions and serve as a colourful side dish with a main of sweet and sour prawns or beef.

Grilled sweet pepper dish

Cut the tops off some peppers and deseed them, then stuff with a mix of cooked couscous, pine nuts, olives, feta cheese, sun-dried tomatoes and basil. Cover with foil and bake in a hot oven for 20 minutes.

Add roasted red and yellow peppers to fried onions, canned plum tomatoes, crushed garlic, and vegetable stock and heat through to make a richly flavoured pasta sauce.

Fruit

A sunny room will provide the ideal growing conditions for a range of fruits such as figs, oranges, and peaches. If you can make space for these handsome plants, they will reward you with fruit and flowers year after year.

Introducing fruit

Grow a **confection of fruits** – strawberries, nectarines, peaches, and exotic and citrus fruits – to bring **summer flavours** and a taste of the **tropics** to your indoor garden.

Exotic flavours

An indoor garden offers you a great opportunity to grow the exotic fruits that struggle to survive outside in harsh winters. Cape gooseberries, for example, are easy to grow on an indoor windowsill and with daily watering will produce their exotic-tasting golden berries with very little fuss. The Brazilian pineapple guava, or feijoa, plant will also grow indoors, producing delicious edible flowers and fruits in warm conditions.

Fresh & fruity

Citrus fruits are not always easy to grow indoors because they require cool temperatures in winter, but if you can provide the right conditions year-round they make wonderful houseplants. Their sweetly fragrant flowers and brightly coloured fruits boost both mind and body: rich in minerals and vitamins, most notably C, they can be used in a wide range of sweet and savoury dishes and drinks. You could also try growing a makrut lime, which is valued in Asian countries for its spicy leaves – typically used in curries and stir-fries – as well as for its knobbly green tangy fruits.

A taste of summer

Soft fruits such as strawberries, and tree fruits such as peaches and nectarines, will thrive in a warm sunny environment. Just remember to hand-pollinate the flowers if you want to enjoy the delicious summery flavours of the fruits, which develop from the blooms. Like citrus, these plants need cool conditions in winter – strawberries will sail through most cold winters on an outside windowsill if you have the space. Packed with vitamins, minerals, and antioxidants, the health benefits of these fruits are greatest when eaten fresh from the plant.

Best zones for fruit

All indoor fruit crops require lots of light and heat to produce their sweet delights, so the best locations to grow them are zones 1, 2, and 3. Most fruit trees also require a cool area in which to overwinter.

South-facing windows
Fruit will ripen well in the hot, sunny conditions close to a south-facing window. Just remember to turn the plants regularly so that all sides receive a good dose of sunlight.

East- and west-facing windows
You should get a good crop of fruit if you locate your fruit plants close to a large east- or west-facing window – as long as it is not shaded by trees or buildings.

Beneath a skylight
These plants will perform well under a skylight, especially if there is some supplementary sunlight from a vertical window. The room may be too hot for wild strawberries.

Walls
Strawberries, especially the wild, or alpine, varieties, will do well on a bright wall out of direct sunlight. The other fruit trees are too large for a wall.

Dark corners
You can try raising strawberries under grow lights. The other, larger, fruit trees are not suitable for domestic grow lights and will suffer in a dark corner.

Centre of a room
Strawberries will perform well here. You may also get fruit from trees in the centre of a sunny, south-facing room, but they will generally fail in other rooms.

Cool (unheated) south-facing room
To produce their fruits each year, citrus trees, figs, peaches, and nectarines must be overwintered in cool or cold conditions such as an unheated room.

Outside windowsill
Strawberries will grow well on outside windowsills, as will Cape gooseberries after all risk of frost has passed. Fruit trees will perform well in summer on a balcony.

Wild strawberry shelves

Diminutive **wild strawberry** plants will grow **happily** in a bright area out of direct sunlight, making them **ideal** for rooms that don't have south-facing windows or a skylight. A shelving unit will **display** them beautifully (see project overleaf).

To overwinter wild strawberry plants, keep them in a cool room or on a sheltered balcony

Growing wild strawberries

These fruiting plants, with sweet berries that are smaller than regular strawberries, are also referred to as alpine or woodland strawberries, where they may often be found growing wild. To ensure your plants produce plenty of fruit indoors, keep them in a bright room that does not get too hot – a temperature of between 16°C and 21°C (61–70°F) is ideal. Relatively trouble-free, they will produce a crop of small, sweet fruits intermittently from early summer – although any strawberry plants grown indoors will need to be hand-pollinated, as explained below.

The small, sweet fruits make a healthy snack for children.

Fruiting wild strawberry (*Fragaria vesca*)

Strawberry care

When the flowers appear, feed the plants fortnightly with high potash fertilizer. In the absence of pollinating insects, you will need to do this job instead. Dust each flower with a clean, soft paint- or make-up brush, transferring pollen from plant to plant so the flowers develop into fruits. For the best crops, do this every few days to ensure all the flowers have been pollinated.

Tickle each little flower with a clean, soft paintbrush every day or two.

Hand-pollinating strawberry plants

Alpine strawberry 'Scarlet Beauty'

The small wild strawberries will appear over many weeks through summer and autumn.

These attractive shelves are made from old wooden fruit or wine crates, and provide just enough space for a few diminutive wild strawberry plants to flourish and produce a crop of small but succulent berries.

Quick growing guide

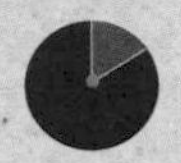

3-4 hours for various stages

Shade for part of the day

Water every 2-3 days

Feed with high potash fertilizer every 2 weeks once the flowers appear

Harvest from early summer

Project >>

YOU WILL NEED

- length of 18mm (3/4in) plywood measuring approximately 75 x 55cm (30 x 22in)
- blackboard paint or emulsion paint
- hand saw
- flat surface such as an old table
- pencil
- wooden batten, 25 x 38mm (1 x 1½in) length dependent on size of crate
- compass for measuring 45° angle
- 1 wooden wine or fruit crate
- electric drill & drill bit
- 16 x M8 crosshead screws 30mm (1¼in) long for the battens and crate
- 4 x M10 crosshead screws 80mm (3in) long for attaching the display to the wall
- 2 heavy-duty black plastic bin liners or waterproof sealant
- 2 coir hanging basket liners
- 8-10 small wild strawberry plants
- multi-purpose compost

Water your strawberries every couple of days so the compost is always moist, but not wet

Make a **wild strawberry** display

You will need just a few basic carpentry skills and tools to transform an **old wooden** wine or vegetable **crate** into this **decorative shelving unit** to display your collection of wild strawberry plants.

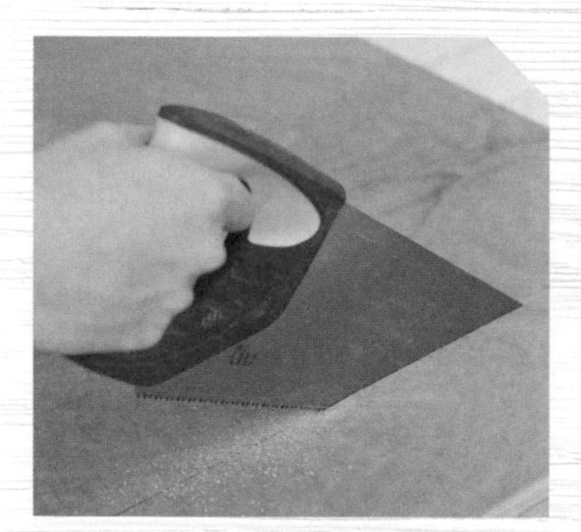

1 With a hand saw, cut the plywood to fit your allocated wall space, while also ensuring that it will accommodate at least two wooden shelves. Apply two coats of blackboard or emulsion paint.

2 Using a pencil and a compass, mark a 45° angle at the bottom front corner of one side of the crate. Using the side of the batten, draw a straight line up to the top edge of the crate. Repeat on the other side.

3 Saw along the line on one side of the crate, and then the other. Prize off this sawn-off section, removing any nails. Repeat at the other end of the crate to create two identical wedge shapes.

4 Lay the back board flat. Centre the two crate ends, one under the other, on the board. Set the batten against the inside edge of one crate end and mark the height of its rim on the batten with a pencil.

5 Cut the batten at a 45° angle along the pencil line. Repeat to make four batten supports that will butt up against each inside edge of the crate ends, as shown above. Mark the positions of the crate ends on the board with the pencil.

6 Using the electric drill, make pilot holes at both ends of each batten. Remove the crate ends from the board. Referring to the marked positions, fix the two battens to the board; check each one is correctly positioned before screwing it in.

7 Repeat with the remaining two battens, then reposition the crate ends over the fixed battens. Using the electric screwdriver, screw the sides of the crate ends, both top and bottom, to the battens with more screws.

8 Secure the back board to the wall with screws at each corner. Line the crate ends – now plant holders – with heavy-duty bin liners or paint on a waterproof sealant. Check they are watertight.

9 Either pop the strawberry plants in their plastic pots inside the plant holders, or line the plant holders with coir basket liner, fill with multi-purpose compost, and plant up the strawberries.

Watering & feeding

Water the strawberry plants sparingly every few days, ensuring that they are moist at all times but don't become waterlogged. When the little flowers appear, hand-pollinate them and start feeding the plants with a high potash fertilizer every two weeks. Buy new strawberry plants every year, or overwinter them in a cool room or outside.

Feed strawberries when flowers appear

Strawberries

Fragaria species

One of the best-loved fruits, strawberries can be grown successfully indoors with a little care and attention. You need to pollinate the plants yourself unless you can set them on an outside window ledge or balcony where insects can reach them.

Strawberry plants will produce crops for two or three years.

'Albion' everbearing strawberry

How to grow

When to buy or sow

Most strawberry plants are available to buy in spring as bare-root or potted plants. You can try raising small wild woodland types by sowing seeds in small pots of seed compost (they may take a few weeks to germinate).

Light & heat

Woodland or alpine berries grow happily in part-shade, such as an east- or west-facing wall or windowsill. Garden strawberries (*Fragaria* x *ananassa*) also grow in low light conditions, but produce more fruits in full sun. The plants enjoy temperatures of 13–21°C (55–70°F).

Watering

Keep well watered. Plant in pots with drainage holes to ensure the compost is never waterlogged, which will cause the plants to rot. Reduce watering in winter.

Aftercare

Feed with high potash fertilizer every week or two as flowers appear. If growing indoors, hand-pollinate the flowers every day or so (p168). If growing outside on a windowsill, cover berries with netting to prevent birds eating them. Remove old stems and withered leaves in winter; plants will send out new growth the following spring.

Harvesting

Pick strawberries when they have coloured up and are soft and sweet. Harvesting the fruits frequently encourages a plant to produce more flowers and fruits.

Firming the soil

Planting bare-root strawberry plants

Once you get the plants (also known as runners) home, soak for 10 minutes, then transplant into a pot with drainage holes filled with good-quality multi-purpose compost or soil-based John Innes no 2. Choose a deep pot so the base of the crown (where the stems meet the roots) is at soil level and the roots extend down without curling upwards – trim to 10cm (4in) if necessary to fit. If the crown is buried or the roots exposed, the plants will not thrive. Water-in over a sink after planting.

Best indoor varieties

There are three types: wild, summer fruiting, and perpetual (everbearing). Wild plants have small fruits, but are tolerant of shade; summer-fruiting types produce heavy crops from early to midsummer; and perpetual varieties produce berries from summer to autumn.

'ALBION' ▲
(*Fragaria* x *ananassa* 'Albion')
Pick the berries of this perpetual-fruiting variety from summer until mid-autumn. It produces dark red fruits with a delicious rich, sweet flavour, and is disease-resistant.
Height & spread:
20 x 30cm (8 x 12in)

'HONEOYE' ▲
(*Fragaria* x *ananassa* 'Honeoye')
The bright red berries of this summer-fruiting variety have a delicious flavour and firm but juicy texture.
Height & spread: 20 x 30cm (8 x 12in)

'SNOW WHITE' ▲
(*Fragaria* x *ananassa* 'Snow White')
Grown in the same ways as ordinary strawberries, the fruits of this unusual white variety with red seeds have a pineapple aroma. If grown outside, the berries are invisible to birds.
Height & spread:
40 x 50cm (16 x 20in)

WILD STRAWBERRY ►
(*Fragaria vesca*)
Fruiting from summer to early autumn, these disease-resistant plants are ideal for growing in pots and hanging baskets.
Height & spread: 20 x 30cm (8 x 12in)

◄ **'FRAU MIEZE SCHINDLER'**
(*Fragaria* x *ananassa* 'Frau Mieze Schindler')
This variety produces a good crop of sweet, exceptional-tasting fruits from early to midsummer.
Height & spread: 30 x 40cm (12 x 16in)

'MARA DES BOIS' ▲
(*Fragaria* x *ananassa* 'Mara des Bois')
Chefs love the superb flavour of the berries of this perpetual-bearing variety. They taste like sweet alpine strawberries and are produced throughout the summer.
Height & spread:
20 x 30cm (8 x 12in)

Cook's tips

Sweet & savoury

For a summery afternoon treat, sandwich a layer of sliced strawberries and thick clotted cream between freshly baked butter shortcake biscuits, top with a couple of strawberry slices, and serve with tea.
Toss sliced strawberries with fresh spinach leaves and almond slivers for a colourful salad.
For fruity ice-lollies, whizz strawberries, natural yoghurt, and honey in a food processor, then pour into moulds and freeze.
Pour strawberry liqueur over wild strawberries, chill overnight, and serve topped with elderflower cream.

Strawberry & cream shortcakes

Quick growing guide

2 hours for various stages

Full sun

Water every day or two

Feed weekly with high potash fertilizer when flowers open

Harvest when strawberries are ripe and flowers appear

Level 1 easy

Fruit & flower windowbox

Pack an **outside windowsill** with a box of **strawberry plants**, peppery **nasturtium flowers** and leaves, and the spicy blooms of **pot marigolds** to use in sweet and savoury salads.

Strawberry flowers are pollinated by insects, which is why they will produce fruit more easily on an outside windowsill

YOU WILL NEED • windowbox • multi-purpose compost • 3 everbearing strawberry plants (see p173 for varieties) • 3 marigold plants (*Calendula officinalis*) • 2 nasturtium plants (*Tropaeolum majus*) • grit, gravel, or crushed seashell mulching material • watering can with rose head

1 Choose a windowbox with drainage holes, or drill several holes in the base. Fill to about 5cm (2in) from the top with multi-purpose compost enriched with fertilizer. Water all the plants well and allow to drain on a draining board.

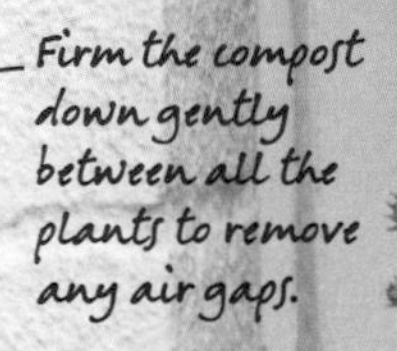

Firm the compost down gently between all the plants to remove any air gaps.

2 Plant the strawberries and nasturtiums alternately at the front of the windowbox. Add the marigolds at the back in between these plants – as they will grow the tallest – and ensure all the roots are covered with compost.

3 Place the windowbox on a draining board and water in the plants to settle the compost around the roots. Add a layer of grit, gravel, or crushed seashells to help lock the moisture in the compost (see also p201), and set the box on an outdoor windowsill.

Pick the blooms from the nasturtiums and marigolds regularly to encourage the plants to produce more flowers.

Create a mix of fruits and flowers in a windowbox for a summer-long display. Keep all the plants in the windowbox well watered, even during wet weather.

Apply a weekly dose of high potash fertilizer as soon as the flowers appear

Quick growing guide

10 minutes to pot up

Full sun 18-24°C (64-75°F) in summer; 8-12°C (46-54°F) in winter

Water every few days in summer; more sparingly in winter

Feed weekly in summer; once a month in winter

Snip mature leaves as needed

Level 2 moderate

Grow your own curry leaves

Spice up your Thai curries and fish dishes with home-grown **makrut lime leaves**. You can use the richly flavoured leaves **fresh or dried** in cooking, and the plant itself will add a touch of visual drama to your interior decor.

Makrut lime leaves

YOU WILL NEED • makrut (or kaffir) lime plant • large plastic pot • citrus compost • container at least 30cm (12in) deep, 18cm (7in) wide • citrus fertilizers • watering can

1 Tip the plant gently out of its pot, and if the roots are very congested around the sides, repot it in a slightly larger plastic container using citrus compost (see pp182-83 for repotting tips). Water well and place the potted lime plant in a decorative container. Feed as explained on p178 and p180, or use a slow-release fertilizer (left).

2 A makrut lime plant needs a bright, sunny spot in summer. In winter, keep it in a cool but bright room. Maintain a humid atmosphere by placing the plant pot on a saucer of gravel or hydroleca filled with water, and add some moss over the top of the compost to help lock in moisture.

Snip off the fresh double-lobed leaves as you need them, or cut off a stem and air-dry the leaves.

3 Harvest the leaves when the plant is in full growth from spring to autumn, but leave the plant in winter when growth will be slow. Use the foliage fresh or cut off and hang a whole stem upside down to dry the leaves, then store them in an airtight container. You can also freeze the fresh leaves.

Makrut lime trees will grow into large plants, so check that you have enough space to accommodate one in a bright room in your home before buying it.
Grow a chilli plant with your lime as two spicy ingredients; both like bright sunlight
Only remove a stem, or a few mature leaves from the tips of the stems, at any one time.
Overwatering can kill a lime plant. If the compost feels wet, tip out any excess water and leave the plant to dry off.

Lemons & limes

Citrus species

Zesty lemons and limes are versatile fruits and the key ingredients in many drinks, desserts, and savoury dishes. To grow them at home, try to mimic their native Mediterranean conditions.

Lemon trees need at least six hours of direct sunlight for the fruits to ripen.

Meyer lemon

How to grow

When to buy or sow

You can buy lemon and lime trees at any time of year, but by purchasing those with some fruit already developing on the stems, you can be sure the plant will be productive. Citrus plants like slightly acidic soil – use special citrus compost or a 50:50 mix of ericaceous and soil-based compost. The pot size depends on the size of the plant, but most plants need a container that is at least 30cm (12in) deep and 18cm (7in) wide.

Light & heat

Both lemon and lime trees need plenty of sunlight in summer and winter, and will thrive in a bright, south-facing room. They require cool winter temperatures – a bright but unheated spare room or conservatory is ideal – and may not fruit until they have undergone this colder period. They will enjoy being outside on a balcony or roof terrace in summer, if you have one.

Watering

Keep the compost moist, but not wet. Stand the pot on a saucer of gravel filled with water to maintain a moist atmosphere, and mist the plant with rain- or filtered water every few days from spring to autumn.

Aftercare

Feed once a month from mid-autumn to mid-spring with a diluted winter citrus granular fertilizer, and every week thereafter with a summer citrus fertilizer. See p206 for advice on pruning.

Best indoor varieties

There are several varieties of lemon and lime you can try at home. The best for growing indoors all year round are compact types, which are grafted on a dwarf rootstock. A specialist nursery can advise you on those that may be suitable for your space. Here are some recommended varieties.

◀ KEY LIME
(*Citrus* x *aurantiifolia*)
Compact enough for a small apartment, even a relatively young plant produces juicy limes. Key limes are more tender than lemon plants.
Size of fruit: approx 5cm (2in)

MAKRUT (KAFFIR) LIME ▶
(*Citrus hystrix*)
Both the leaves and fruits are used in many Asian dishes. The plants are fairly easy to grow, and tolerate slightly higher winter temperatures. **Size of fruit:** approx 8–10cm (3–4in)

TAHITI LIME ▲
(*Citrus* x *latifolia*)
Sometimes called the Persian or Bearss lime, the fruits are like those you buy in the shops and are ideal for adding to drinks and desserts. The plants produce seedless fruits throughout the year. Look for a lime tree grafted on a dwarf stock such as 'PS'.
Size of fruit: approx 5–6cm (2–2½in)

MEYER LEMON ▲
(*Citrus* x *limon* 'Meyer')
A compact lemon tree rarely growing to more than 1.8m (6ft) in height. The plants produce thick-skinned fruits with a classic lemon flavour.
Size of fruit: approx 8–10cm (3–4in)

Citrus suggestions

Rich in vitamin C, lemons and limes make fresh-tasting accompaniments to many drinks and cocktails.
Squeeze the juice of several lemons and limes and add water and sugar to taste for a zingy cordial.
Mix the zest of a lemon with some butter and chopped fresh rosemary and push it beneath the skin of a chicken. Place the lemon inside the chicken cavity and roast for the recommended time.

Wash the salty preserved lemons before using in dishes.

When to harvest

Lemons and limes produce flowers in late spring, and the fruits then develop over the next six to 12 months. This means that there are often fragrant flowers on the plant at the same time as mature fruits. Lemon fruits are ripe as soon as they turn yellow and have a glossy appearance. Limes turn yellow when ripe, but would be picked when still green and firm.

Picking & storing

The fruits often mature at different rates over a month or two, rather than all at once, which means you will rarely have a glut, particularly on a small tree.

Snip off the fruits with sharp scissors or secateurs, or cup the fruit in your hand and twist it gently until it breaks off the tree. Once harvested, use them fresh, store for up to two weeks in the fridge, or cut into slices and freeze – an ideal way to preserve them for summery drinks.

Preserving in jars

Try storing a few small lemons in a large sterilized Kilner jar filled with herbs and spices, and covered with salted lemon juice. Allow to cure for a few weeks and top up with more lemon juice if needed. Use in tagines and other chicken dishes.

Level 2 moderate

Oranges in pots for a sunny room

Little **calamondin oranges** and **kumquats** fruit well when grown indoors in a bright sunlit room (see project overleaf). Calamondins are perfect for **making marmalade**, and you can **eat** both the skin and flesh of kumquat fruits.

YOU WILL NEED • tray • gravel or hydroleca • citrus or ericaceous compost • summer & winter citrus fertilizers • Epsom salts • sequestered iron • mister

Watering & feeding

Citrus plants prefer acidic soil conditions, so if your water is "hard" and contains alkaline calcium, you should ideally water the plants with rain- or filtered water. Allow the plants to almost dry out in winter, but keep the compost moist at all times from spring to autumn. They also need to be fed regularly with citrus fertilizers designed for summer and winter growth (see overleaf). Misting them weekly with a 50:50 mix of Epsom salts and sequestered iron diluted in water will also keep the plants in good health.

The fruits take almost a year to mature, so the plant often fruits and flowers at the same time

Creating an ideal environment

To maintain a humid atmosphere around your plant during the warmer seasons, plant it in a pot with a drainage hole and set it on a tray filled with gravel or hydroleca and water. Calamondins and kumquats enjoy bright sun and warmth in summer but need a cool area in winter, such as an unheated conservatory, spare room, or porch.

Comprised of small water-absorbing clay pebbles, hydroleca will help to create a humid atmosphere around your plant.

Display your kumquat and calamondin plants next to a bright sunny window or under a skylight. Keep your citrus plants away from radiators, electric heaters, and open fires.

Ripe kumquat fruits can be harvested from the plants over many weeks from late winter.

Quick growing guide

30 minutes to repot

Full sun 18-24°C (64-75°F) in summer; 8-12°C (46-54°F) in winter

Water every few days in summer; more sparingly in winter

Feed weekly in summer; once a month in winter

Harvest the fruits when ripe

Project >>

Repot a calamondin orange

Container-grown calamondins can grow up to 1.8 metres (6ft) or more in height and will need **repotting** in spring **every year or two** as they mature to keep them healthy. Do this very carefully if the plant is still in fruit, or harvest the little oranges before you begin.

Oranges are greedy fruits and need feeding every week from spring to autumn, and once every four weeks during the winter

YOU WILL NEED • plastic pot one size bigger than the original pot • citrus or ericaceous compost • citrus summer fertilizer • watering can or jug

Repot kumquats and other orange plants in spring using this same method

1 Water your calamondin well and leave to drain in the kitchen sink an hour or two before repotting it. Cover the base of the larger plastic pot with a thin layer of citrus compost. Alternatively, use a mix of ericaceous and multi-purpose compost.

2 Carefully tip the calamondin out of its pot, holding it gently by its central stem. Place the plant in the new pot and check that the top of the rootball is sitting just below the rim.

3 Add or remove compost from the bottom to achieve the right level. Then fill in around the sides of the plant with more compost, firming it with your fingers to remove any air gaps.

4 After repotting, feed the calamondin using a summer citrus fertilizer, taking care to measure the powder out carefully before diluting to ensure you apply the correct dosage.

5 Place the plastic pot in a decorative container, and water and mist the plant every couple of days in summer. Reduce the frequency of watering to once a week in the winter months to allow the top of the compost to dry out before watering again.

Oranges

Citrus species

Their colourful fruits and perfumed flowers make oranges popular indoor plants; most produce a crop in late winter or early spring, when few other homegrown fruits are ready.

How to grow

When to buy or sow

Orange trees are available to buy at any time of year. If the roots are congested, repot in citrus compost, as described on pp182–83.

Light & heat

As well as requiring natural sunlight, oranges also need cool indoor temperatures in winter (similar to their native Mediterranean climate), to ensure the fruits set. A sunny, unheated bright spare room or conservatory is ideal during the winter months. In summer, keep in a warm, sunny area and open the windows to increase the ventilation.

Watering

Keep the compost moist, but not wet, and reduce watering in winter. Stand your potted orange on a saucer of gravel and water to maintain a humid atmosphere.

Aftercare

Feed an orange plant once a month from autumn to mid-spring with a winter citrus fertilizer, and weekly for the rest of the year with a summer citrus fertilizer.

Harvesting

The ripe fruits can be left on the plant for a few weeks until you are ready to eat them. Snip off each fruit carefully with secateurs.

Best indoor varieties

Buy naturally small trees, such as mandarins and kumquats, or oranges grown on dwarf rootstocks, but remember that even these will grow to 1.8m (6ft) in height or more over time.

◀ SWEET ORANGE
(*Citrus sinensis*)
Buy a plant on a dwarf rootstock, and enjoy the large sweet fruits, which are similar to those you buy in the shops.
Size of fruit: approx 10cm (4in)

MANDARIN ORANGE ▶
(*Citrus reticulata*)
These small trees produce crops of pebble-skinned, easy-to-peel sweet fruits.
Size of fruit: approx 6cm (2 ½in)

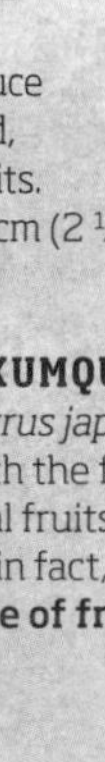

◀ KUMQUAT
(*Citrus japonica*)
Both the flesh and skin of the oval fruits can be eaten; the skin is, in fact, sweeter than the flesh.
Size of fruit: approx 6cm (2 ½in)

CALAMONDIN ▶
(x *Citrofortunella microcarpa*)
One of the easiest oranges to grow indoors, even young plants will produce a bumper crop of small, bitter fruits, ideal for making marmalade.
Size of fruit: 5–6cm (2–2½in)

Oranges need plenty of natural sunlight all year round and good ventilation in summer

Calamondin orange

Sweet & savoury

Drizzle peeled orange slices with rosewater and honey. Top with cinnamon, pomegranate seeds, pistachios and mint leaves.

Make a salad of mandarin segments tossed with toasted almonds, mixed salad greens and crumbled Gorgonzola cheese.

Wrap marinated king prawns around whole kumquats, thread onto skewers, then grill.

Create a refreshing tropical fruit salad by combining bite-sized chunks of orange, grapefruit, pineapple, and melon with black grapes and pomegranate seeds.

Fresh fruit salad

Either set your fig on a table or stool – or the floor if the plant is big – near a patio door or a full-length window so that it receives the maximum amount of light.

Fruity fig tree

A fig tree makes a **dramatic houseplant** with its handsome sculptural leaves and elegant shape, but if you can encourage yours to produce a crop of deliciously **sweet fruits** too, this decorative tree will **earn its keep** (see project overleaf).

Making space for figs

Figs (*Ficus carica*) naturally grow into large shrubs or trees, but by restricting their roots in a pot you can keep them much smaller, although a mature plant may still reach 1.2m (4ft) in height and 1m (3ft) in diameter, or more. Like citrus plants, figs prefer a warm, bright, sunny location in summer, and a cooler, unheated room in winter, when the plant will shed its leaves (and can then tolerate shadier conditions, too).

Figs are not actually fruits, but a hollow stem that contains many flowers and seeds

Choosing a fig for your home

Select a fig from a garden centre that has been raised in a pot and already has a few fruit buds or more mature figs developing on the stems. You can buy plants pre-trained into a vase shape or a standard with a clear lower stem and ball-shaped upper growth. Alternatively, buy a cheaper plant and train it yourself (p207).

'Violette de Sollies' fruits have scented flesh.

'Violette de Sollies'
The large dark purple fruits of this variety are almost black in colour when fully ripe, while the unusual leaves have fine serrated edges. The figs are ready to harvest from late summer to autumn.

Brunswick
The large green-skinned fruits ripen early and have a rich, sweet flavour. This variety survives on a balcony outside all year in mild climates.

'Brown Turkey'
This popular outdoor variety grows equally well indoors, and produces heavy crops of large brown fruits with sweet red flesh. Restrict its growth by pruning back long stems.

Pick figs when they are slightly soft.

Quick growing guide

2-3 hours for various stages

Full sun or part shade

Water every 1-3 days from spring to autumn; once a week in winter

Feed weekly with high potash fertilizer when fruits appear

Harvest when fruits are ripe in late summer

Project >>

Grow a fig for your home

Most fig trees yield a crop of **ripe fruits** from **late summer** to **mid-autumn**, and require a little care throughout the year to produce this sweet harvest. Potting them on into increasingly larger containers encourages **optimum growth**, while selective **pruning** will increase their **productivity**.

In spring, cut out spindly stems to leave only the thick stems that produce the fruits

YOU WILL NEED • decorative container with drainage holes • drip tray • soil-based compost, such as John Innes no 3 • horticultural grit • slow-release all-purpose granular fertilizer • seaweed foliar fertilizer • watering can • pot trolley (optional) • secateurs

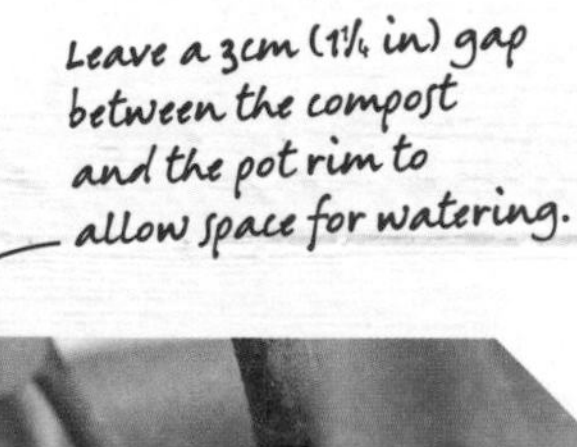

1 Fig trees produce their best crops of fruit when their roots are restricted, but they still need to be potted on into larger containers every year in spring. Choose a pot 5–8cm (2–3in) wider and 2.5–5cm (1–2in) deeper than the original.

2 Add a layer of soil-based compost mixed with a handful of horticultural grit to the larger container. Remove the fig from its pot and gently tease out any tightly packed roots, which will encourage them to grow into the fresh compost.

3 Place the plant in the container and fill in around the rootball with compost. Mix slow-release all-purpose granular fertilizer into the top layer of compost, cover any exposed granules, and firm down with your fingers to remove air gaps.

4 Place the pot on a waterproof tray close to a sunny window or under a bright skylight. Water every few days from spring to autumn when the plant is in full growth so that the compost is always damp, but never wet.

5 Six to eight weeks after planting, feed the fig every fortnight with a foliar seaweed fertilizer, which helps to strengthen the leaves and protect the plant against pests and diseases. Apply a high potash feed when fruits form.

6 Turn the fig around every week or two if it is growing next to a window to ensure all sides receive adequate sunlight. Water your fig every day when the temperatures rise in summer and the fruits are setting.

Pruning

Regular pruning keeps a fig healthy. In winter, remove dead and diseased stems (these look darker and may be brittle) down to clean white wood. Remove any wayward growth that spoils the plant's shape. In late spring, cut off the growing tips of the new season's growth to leave stems with 4–5 leaves. In mid-autumn, remove green figs larger than a pea in size, but leave smaller fruitlets, produced in late summer, which will survive winter and become mature fruits the following summer. Fruitlets that grow in spring may also ripen in autumn.

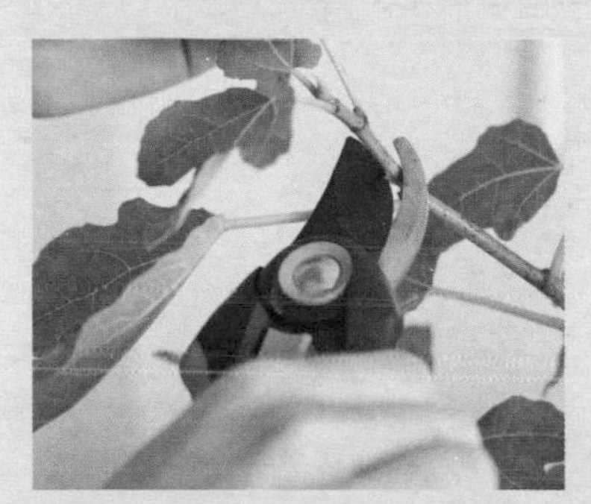

Late-spring pruning
Remove the growing tips of each branch in late spring to encourage fruit to grow. Cut just above a leaf stem or fruitlet.

Autumn pruning
After the fig loses its leaves, remove all unripe fruits from the tree apart from those that are about the size of a pea.

Peaches & nectarines

Prunus persica

These fruit trees will grow successfully indoors if you have a warm sunny area for them to bask in during the summer, and a cooler room to overwinter them. These closely related species are grown in the same way.

'Bonanza' peach

How to grow

When to buy or sow

Buy a self-fertile tree in early to mid-spring, either already potted up or as a bare-root specimen. Check that the one you buy is grafted on a compact rootstock; ask the nursery for advice if you are unsure. If you buy a bare-root tree, soak the roots for 10 minutes when you get it home and pot it up in a container at least 45cm (18in) in diameter filled with soil-based compost such as John Innes no 3. Ensure the container has drainage holes and a saucer or tray underneath it, or stand it in a slightly larger waterproof pot. Don't add any fertilizer at this stage.

Light & heat

Peach and nectarine trees need lots of light from spring to early autumn, and require a spot close to a large south-facing window and/or under a bright skylight. If you grow them next to a window, turn the pot every week or two to promote even growth. In winter, keep these deciduous plants cool in an unheated room or on a sheltered balcony. They won't require as much light at this time of year.

Watering

Keep the compost moist at all times during the growing season from spring to early autumn. Try to water your peach or nectarine consistently, as irregular watering when the fruits are ripening can result in split skins. Reduce watering in winter; once a week should be fine in a cool room.

Aftercare

When peaches flower, pollinate them by dabbing the bristles of a small clean paintbrush into each bloom every day or two. Misting the blooms also helps the fruit to set. Feed the plants every fortnight with a high potash fertilizer when the flowers appear. When the fruits are the size of a hazelnut, thin them to one every 10cm (4in), and again to one every 20–25cm (8–10in) when walnut-sized. When the fruits are about the size of a small cherry tomato, remove any that are misshapen or showing signs of disease. Each spring, mix a granular all-purpose fertilizer into the compost, and repot plants with compacted roots every 2–3 years in a slightly larger container filled with John Innes no 3 compost.

Harvesting

Pick peach and nectarine fruits only when they're fully ripe: cup each fruit lightly in your hand and gently lift to release it from the stem.

Hand-pollinate flowers
Replicate the process of pollination by using a paintbrush to hand-pollinate your indoor blooms (p207).

Fruit ripening on branch
Check ripening fruit regularly and remove any that show signs of disease.

Best varieties

Choose a naturally dwarf peach or nectarine plant variety or one grafted on a compact rootstock; a specialist nursery will be able to advise you.

Peaches have furry skins, while the skins of nectarines are smooth.

◀ **'AVALON PRIDE'**
(*Prunus persica* 'Avalon Pride')
The self-fertile trees produce pretty pink flowers followed by sweet, juicy fruits from late summer to early autumn.
Height & spread: up to 1.8 x 1.2m (6 x 4ft)

'BONANZA' ▲
(*Prunus persica* 'Bonanza')
This self-fertile patio peach tree is naturally dwarf, yet it produces full-sized juicy fruits. It requires little or no pruning to keep its compact shape.
Height & spread: 70–80cm (28–32in)

◀ **'LORD NAPIER'**
(*Prunus persica* var. *nectarina* 'Lord Napier')
This nectarine tree produces yellow-flushed red flesh with an excellent sweet flavour in late summer.
Height & spread: 1.8 x 1.2m (6 x 4ft)

Cook's tips

Peachy delights

Toss stoned peach halves with salad greens, crispy prosciutto, feta cheese, and toasted walnuts for a simple summer salad.
Thread cubes of peach and pork onto skewers, drizzle with lemon juice and honey, and grill until cooked.
Top rectangles of puff pastry with *crème pâtissière* and halved stoned peaches. Bake in a hot oven for 10–15 minutes for an easy tart.
Serve sliced nectarines with ricotta and goat's cheese topped with toasted almonds and honey.
Bake peach slices until soft, drizzle with honey, sprinkle with pistachios, and grill until browned on top.

Peach & nectarine puff pastry tart

Pineapple guavas

Acca sellowiana

This small evergreen shrub produces exotic-looking edible flowers and green oval fruits, sometimes known as feijoas, which are sweet, aromatic, and taste a little like kiwi fruit. The plants like warm conditions for most of the year.

How to grow

When to buy or sow

You can buy the plants from specialist nurseries at any time of the year, but you are more likely to reap a crop of fruits if you buy a plant in flower in late spring. You also need two plants to cross fertilize if you want fruits. Plant in pots with drainage holes and fill with soil-based compost mixed with horticultural grit. Stand the pots on saucers or place inside watertight containers.

Light & heat

Although these plants are from Brazil and require a bright spot and heat to produce their green fruits, they need a cooler situation, such as an unheated spare room, for a few weeks in winter. (The plants are, in fact, hardy down to -12°C/10°F and can be set on a roof terrace or balcony, if you have one, in winter).

Long stamens protrude from the flowers.

Pineapple guava in flower

Watering

Pineapple guavas are drought-tolerant plants and will suffer if over-watered, so check that the compost never becomes too wet. However, they need constant moisture, especially when the flowers appear and the fruits are developing.

Aftercare

Apply a high potash fertilizer every week once the flowers appear and until all the fruits have ripened in late summer or early autumn. You may also have to hand-pollinate the flowers to ensure they produce fruits.

Hand-pollinate the flowers by dabbing a clean paintbrush onto the stamens (with red stalks) and carpel (central section of the flower) every few days, ensuring you "tickle" them all

Harvesting

The fruits will fall off the plant when ripe, although to prevent any bruising you can gently squeeze them to check they are soft just before they fall and cut them from the plant. You can also harvest the edible flowers and use as a garnish (see right).

EXOTIC FRUITS
Pineapple guava fruits can be sliced and included in fruit salads, or scoop out the pulp and use it in smoothies or as a fruity topping on yogurt.

The plant flowers in early summer and produces exotic-looking white and pink flowers with fleshy edible petals.

Pineapple guava plant

Exotic touches

Add the flowers, which have a sweet, fruity flavour, to an iced cake as a stunning floral decoration.

For an exotic fruit salad, slice the guavas, with or without the skin, and add to the fruity confection.

Make a salsa with chopped pineapple guava fruit, onions, fresh coriander, brown sugar, and some freshly ground black pepper.

Scoop out the flesh of some pineapple guava fruits and blitz it in a blender together with some fresh strawberries, apples, and apple juice to make a delicious smoothie.

Fruit smoothie

Cape gooseberries

Physalis peruviana

The velvety leaves and custard yellow lanterns that encase the sweet golden "gooseberries" make these indoor edible plants stand out from the crowd. Easy to care for, they will thrive in a warm, sunlit room.

How to grow

When to buy or sow

These plants need a long growing period to produce fruits. If growing from seed, sow in late winter in pots of good-quality seed compost and cover them lightly with vermiculite (p204). Alternatively, buy young plants from a garden centre in the spring and plant up in soil-based compost such as John Innes no 2 or multi-purpose compost.

Light & heat

Cape gooseberry seeds need a temperature of 18–21°C (64–70°F) to germinate. Place the seedlings and plants in a sunny position, for example on a south-facing windowsill. The mature plants will tolerate a minimum temperature of 15°C (59°F) or a little lower at night.

Watering

These plants need plenty of moisture, so water them every day to prevent them from wilting, especially after the flowers start to form. However, make sure the compost never becomes waterlogged by planting them in pots with drainage holes.

Aftercare

Continue to pot up the plants into increasingly larger containers as they grow, and feed them every fortnight with a high potash fertilizer when the flowers appear. The stems may require staking too. The plants will overwinter in a cool room.

Harvesting

Cut off the lanterns in autumn when they are brittle and pale brown in colour and the fruits inside are golden orange. Store the fruits in their husks for up to a month at room temperature.

FLOWERS ▶
The pretty yellow flowers with maroon blotches in the centre don't need to be hand-pollinated, but you can spray the blooms every few days with a water mister to encourage the fruits to set.

The pretty blooms are self-fertilizing.

The nutritious sweet berries are rich in vitamins A and C and iron.

Ripe fruits

FABULOUS FRUITS ▶
After the flowers appear, tiny green "lanterns" start to develop. These gradually turn to yellow and then become crisp and brittle, indicating that the berries inside are ripe.

◀ LITTLE LANTERNS For indoor displays, choose a compact variety such as 'Little Lanterns', which will grow to around 90cm (36in) in height.

Sweet treats

Dip Cape gooseberries and strawberries in melted chocolate, allow to cool and set, and serve as an after-dinner sweet.
Mix a few berries with apples to inject a flavour bomb into a crumble.
Blend Cape gooseberries with honey and water until smooth, strain, then freeze in an ice cube tray. Add the frozen cubes to tall glasses of coconut milk and serve.
Make a salad from halved Cape gooseberries, chopped cucumber, chopped fresh coriander, grilled sweetcorn, and toasted sesame seeds.

Chocolate-coated Cape gooseberries & strawberries

Expert's tips

The advice in this chapter on basic plant care, such as watering, feeding, and pruning, will help you keep your indoor crops healthy and productive, while preserving tips offer great ways to make the most of your indoor edibles.

Planning your indoor edible gardening year

Harvesting symbols
- ❋ harvest flowers
- ♂ harvest fruits
- ❦ harvest leaves
- ⁂ harvest shoots
- ♁ harvest bulbs
- ✱ harvest roots

This planner will help you to **produce** a **year-round** indoor edible garden, showing what to **sow** and **plant** through the **seasons**, and when you can expect a **harvest** from the crops in this book. Although most plants grow from **spring to autumn** when conditions are optimum, remember that you can still enjoy fresh salad leaves, sprouts, and fruits (such as citrus), in **winter** when light levels and temperatures are lower.

EARLY TO MID-SPRING

Sow seed

Aubergine
Basil
Beetroot
Carrot
Chilli pepper
Chives
Cucamelon
Cucumber
Garlic greens
Lettuce
Microgreens
Mizuna & mibuna
Pak choi
Parsley
Pot marigold
Radish
Spring onion
Sprouts
Sweet pepper
Tomato
Viola

Plant young plants/bulbs

Bellis daisy
Calamondin
Cape gooseberry
Chives
Fig
Garlic greens
Kumquat
Lavender
Lemon & lime
Lettuce
Mint
Mizuna & mibuna
Orange
Orchid: Dendrobium
Pak choi
Parsley
Peach & nectarine
Pineapple guava
Primrose
Radish
Rosemary
Sage
Spring onion
Strawberry
Thyme
Tulip
Viola

Harvest

Bellis daisy ❋
Calamondin ♂
Chives ❦
Kumquat ♂
Lemon & lime ♂
Lettuce ❦
Microgreens ❦
Mint ❦
Mizuna & mibuna ❦
Mushroom
Orange ♂
Orchid: Dendrobium ❋
Pak choi ❦
Parsley ❦
Primrose ❋
Rosemary ❦
Sage ❦
Sprouts ⁂
Thyme ❦
Tulip ❋
Viola ❋

LATE SPRING

Sow seed

Basil
Beetroot
Carrot
Chives
Cucamelon
Cucumber
Lettuce
Microgreens
Mizuna & mibuna
Nasturtium
Pak choi
Parsley
Pot marigold
Radish
Spring onion
Sprouts
Tomato

Plant young plants/bulbs

Aubergine
Basil
Beetroot
Bellis daisy
Calamondin
Cape gooseberry
Carrot
Chilli pepper
Chives
Cucamelon
Cucumber
Fig
Garlic greens
Kumquat
Lavender
Lemon & lime
Lemon verbena
Lettuce
Mint
Mizuna & mibuna
Nasturtium
Orange
Orchid (Dendrobium)
Pak choi
Parsley
Peach & nectarine
Pineapple guava
Pot marigold
Primrose
Radish
Rosemary
Sage
Spring onion
Stevia
Strawberry
Sweet pepper
Thyme
Tomato
Tulip
Viola

Harvest

Bellis daisies ❋
Calamondin ♂
Chives ❦
Kumquat ♂
Lemon & lime ♂
Lemon verbena ❦
Microgreens ❦
Mint ❦
Mushroom
Orange ♂
Orchid: Dendrobium ❋
Parsley ❦
Primrose ❋
Rosemary ❦
Sage ❦
Sprouts ⁂
Stevia ❦
Thyme ❦
Tulip ❋
Viola ❋

EARLY SUMMER

Sow seed

Basil
Carrot
Chives
Lettuce
Microgreens
Mizuna & mibuna
Pak choi
Parsley
Pot marigold
Radish
Spring onion
Sprouts

Plant young plants/bulbs

Aubergine
Basil
Beetroot
Calamondin
Cape gooseberry
Carrot
Chilli pepper
Chives
Cucamelon
Cucumber
Fig
Garlic greens
Kumquat
Lavender
Lemon & lime
Lemon verbena
Lettuce
Mint
Mizuna & mibuna
Nasturtium
Orange
Orchid: Dendrobium
Pak choi
Parsley
Peach & nectarine
Pineapple guava
Pot marigold
Radish
Rosemary
Sage
Spring onion
Stevia
Strawberry
Sweet pepper
Tomato
Thyme
Viola

Harvest

Basil
Carrot
Chives
Garlic greens
Lemon verbena
Lettuce
Microgreens
Mint
Mizuna & mibuna
Mushroom
Nasturtium
Orchid: Dendrobium
Pak choi
Parsley
Radish
Rosemary
Sage
Spring onions
Sprouts
Stevia
Strawberry
Thyme
Tulip
Viola

MID- to LATE SUMMER

Sow seed

Lettuce
Microgreens
Pak choi
Radish
Sprouts

Plant young plants/bulbs

Basil
Calamondin
Chives
Garlic greens
Kumquat
Lavender
Lemon & lime
Lemon verbena
Lettuce
Mint
Mizuna & mibuna
Nasturtium
Orange
Parsley
Peach & nectarine
Pineapple guava
Pot marigold
Radish
Rosemary
Sage
Spring onion
Stevia
Thyme

Harvest

Aubergine
Basil
Beetroot
Cape gooseberry
Carrot
Chilli pepper
Chives
Cucamelon
Cucumber
Fig
Garlic greens
Lavender
Lemon verbena
Lettuce
Microgreens
Mint
Mizuna & mibuna
Mushroom
Nasturtium
Pak choi
Parsley
Peach & nectarine
Pineapple guava
Pot marigold
Radish
Rosemary
Sage
Spring onion
Sprouts
Stevia
Strawberry
Sweet pepper
Thyme
Tomato
Viola

AUTUMN

Sow seed

Lettuce
Microgreens
Mizuna & mibuna
Pak choi
Sprouts
Viola

Plant

Calamondin
Garlic greens
Kumquat
Lavender
Lemon & lime
Orange
Peach & nectarine
Pineapple guava
Rosemary
Sage
Stevia
Thyme

Harvest

Aubergine
Basil
Beetroot
Cape gooseberry
Carrot
Chilli pepper
Chives
Cucamelon
Cucumber
Garlic greens
Lemon verbena
Lettuce
Microgreens
Mint
Mizuna & mibuna
Mushroom
Nasturtium
Pak choi
Parsley
Pineapple guava
Radish
Rosemary
Sage
Sprouts
Stevia
Sweet pepper
Thyme
Tomato
Viola

WINTER

Sow seed

Cape gooseberry
Lettuce
Microgreens
Mizuna & mibuna
Pak choi
Sprouts
Viola

Plant

Calamondin
Kumquat
Lemon & lime
Orange
Peach & nectarine
Pineapple guava
Rosemary
Sage
Thyme

Harvest

Calamondin
Kumquat
Lemon & lime
Lettuce
Microgreens
Mizuna & mibuna
Mushroom
Orange
Pak choi
Sprouts
Viola

Choosing the **right compost**

With such a vast array of compost types available to buy, choosing the right one for a particular crop can be confusing. This guide explains which **plants grow best** in the **different composts** and growing media that you will find in your local garden centre.

Multi-purpose compost

Also known as all-purpose compost, this lightweight type is available to buy with or without peat. You can also buy organic multi-purpose composts, which contain plant or tree derivatives that have been certified organic. Most of these composts are made from natural materials, such as coir, bark, and composted wood fibre. Many also contain added fertilizers, which will feed the crops for the first few weeks after you have planted them.

Best for: annual crops that will not be in a pot for more than a year; hanging baskets.

Seed & cutting compost

As the name suggests, this is the best compost choice for growing crops from seed. It has a finer texture than many other types, which means that even tiny seeds will be in contact with the compost, thereby aiding germination. It is also free-draining, but low in nutrients (the formula is not rich enough to sustain mature plants). Most seed and cutting composts contain a mixture of peat, loam (soil), grit, and sand.

Best for: sowing seeds in pots and trays; potting up cuttings and young seedlings.

Soil- or loam-based compost

Also known as "John Innes" compost, this type contains sterilized soil, which is similar in structure to garden soil. John Innes no 3 is ideal for mature plants, such as fruit trees, which will grow on in their pots for a few years. Take care when carrying bags of soil-based compost since it contains grit and sand, which makes it very heavy. Many soil-based composts also contain fertilizers.

Best for: perennial crops, such as fruit trees and shrubs, which will remain in the same pot for more than one year.

Some composts are designed specifically for vegetables or certain types of plant, such as citrus

Ericaceous compost

This type is similar to multi-purpose compost, but designed for plants such as oranges, lemons, and limes that require acidic soil conditions. It is carefully formulated to include all the nutrients these plants require, but it is best mixed with a soil-based compost for trees and shrubs (left). Remember, too, that you will need to top up the nutrients with a fertilizer for acid-loving plants when those in the compost are depleted.

Best for: lemon, lime, kumquat, calamondin, and orange plants.

Aggregates & other materials

You will also find a range of other products for sale that can help your plants to thrive. These include decorative mulching materials, which can be added as a layer on top of compost to help retain moisture, and grit and gravel, which aid drainage when mixed with compost or added to the bottom of a pot.

Mulches ▶

This material is spread in a layer over the top of compost to prevent its surface drying out quickly and to lock in the moisture available to plants' roots. Mulches can be made of organic material, such as wood chips or compost, or aggregates - gravel, crushed seashells, glass chips, and other recycled products.

Some mulches are designed to also look decorative.

◀ Vermiculite & perlite

Vermiculite is a mineral heated to produce lightweight, spongy grains, while perlite is a volcanic rock, also heated to form similar white-grey absorbent grains. Both hold onto moisture, then release it slowly. They can be mixed with compost or used to cover small seeds, keeping them moist while allowing light through to aid germination.

Perlite, like vermiculite, releases water into the compost.

Horticultural gravel & grit ▶

A layer of gravel in the base of a waterproof pot creates a reservoir for water to drain into, supports the plant roots and compost above, and helps to prevent waterlogging. Grit mixed with compost increases drainage and provides good growing conditions for drought-loving plants such as Mediterranean herbs.

These aggregates are pre-washed and safe to use for indoor projects.

Watering & feeding indoor edibles

Healthy plants produce the best crops, so it pays to **water** and **feed** them **well**. To do this effectively, you need to give the plants **just the right amount** of each. To ensure your crops **thrive indoors**, follow these tips to provide them with the **perfect levels** of food and water.

Watering know-how

All crops need the right amount of moisture to feed their roots, and to produce a good crop of leaves, fruits, or flowers. The trick to growing indoor crops successfully is to supply them with plenty of water while avoiding soggy compost, which may cause stems to rot and encourages some fungal diseases. To do this, ensure your crops are planted in pots with drainage holes in the base (or with an integral drainage system, below), and set these pots inside waterproof containers or on saucers. To test the compost moisture level, feel the surface and poke your finger about 2cm (3/4in) down into the soil. If it feels dry, pour on some water. If the top of the compost is wet and glistening with moisture, it may be waterlogged. Drain any excess from the waterproof pot, and don't water the plant again for a day or two until the top of the compost feels dry.

Watering from below
One way to ensure you don't flood a plant with too much water and cause spillages is to pour the water into the saucer beneath the pot. The compost then draws the moisture up through the drainage holes to the plant's roots.

Prevent waterlogging
Some containers for indoor use may incorporate a plastic plate on supports that creates a well in the base to minimize the risk of waterlogged compost.

Avoid fungal infection
Water the compost only, not the plant's leaves, flowers, or fruits, as it can encourage diseases such as grey mould and downy mildew (p209).

Use a rose head
Use a watering can fitted with a rose head to water all seedlings and young plants, which may otherwise be dislodged by a stream of water.

Food for thought

Edible plants need a range of nutrients to keep them healthy; the most important are nitrogen (N), potassium (K) – or potash, as it is often called – and phosphorous (P). These nutrients promote the health and development of different parts of a plant: nitrogen encourages healthy leaf growth; potash stimulates a plant to flower and fruit; and phosphorous helps it develop strong roots. Most all-purpose fertilizers contain a balance of the key nutrients as well as essential micro-nutrients, but others, such as those for leafy or fruit crops, contain a concentration of nitrogen or potash.

Take care not to over-fertilize your crops, as this can cause more damage than underfeeding them. Fertilizer packs will also specify if they are suitable for organically grown crops.

Follow the recommended dosages on fertilizer packs.

Preparing fertilizer
Many liquid fertilizers and powders will need to be diluted before you apply them to your crops. Check the pack carefully for instructions on how to do this, and do not be tempted to give more than is required.

Fertilizers for long-term crops

Slow-release granular fertilizers that provide nutrients over a number of months can be added to compost when planting. They contain all the vital nutrients needed for healthy plant growth and can be used for crops, such as fruit trees, that will grow in their pots from year to year. For established plants, remove the top layer of compost each spring and replace with some slow-release fertilizer mixed with fresh compost.

Feeding fruit trees
Trees such as figs and peaches benefit from an annual dose of all-purpose slow-release fertilizer to keep them in good health all year. Apply granules as directed on the pack in early spring.

Easy hydroponics

Many commercial crops are now grown without soil using a system known as "hydroponics". This term simply means growing plants in water. The compost or soil is replaced by materials such as coconut husks or pumice stones, which accommodate the roots. Most of the hydroponic systems available require you to have an understanding of the specific nutrient needs of your chosen crop, which you then apply carefully to the plants to ensure good growth (nutrients are naturally present in soils and are added to many composts). Many also include grow lights.

If you are new to hydroponics, look out for complete units that provide everything you need, including the growing unit, seeds, medium, nutrient packs, and a grow light. You can then experiment with more sophisticated systems once you feel confident.

Salad leaves growing in a hydroponic unit

Sowing from seed

The **choice of seeds** for indoor edible crops is much **wider** than the selection of young plants available to buy, so it is well worth giving them a go. **Many plants**, such as **lettuce**, **cucumbers**, and **tomatoes sprout quickly**, too, so you will soon see some results.

Remove any covers as soon as the seeds germinate to prevent damping-off disease, which kills young seedlings

YOU WILL NEED

- seed trays with plastic lids
- seed compost
- vermiculite
- waterproof tray
- plant labels
- watering can with rose head
- multi-purpose compost
- small & larger plastic pots

1 Select a range of seeds to grow and sow one type in each seed tray (do not mix the varieties). Place the seed trays in a waterproof container and fill them almost to the top with good-quality seed compost.

2 Place a spare clean seed tray on top of the compost in the container and press it down gently to create a level surface. Using your fingers, press the compost down around the edges too.

3 Lightly water the compost, just enough to dampen the surface, using a watering can with a fine rose head. Open the seed pack and sow the seeds thinly and evenly in rows on the compost.

A covering of vermiculite is ideal for seeds that need light to germinate.

4 Check the seed pack for the required planting depth for each type of seed. Either cover them to this depth with more compost or with a layer of vermiculite, which helps to keep the seeds moist while allowing light through for germination. Label each tray.

5 Place plastic lids over the trays of seeds and set in a warm place such as a sunny windowsill. (Some seeds germinate faster if placed in a propagator.) Keep the seeds moist by watering into the waterproof container beneath – the compost will draw up the moisture and when you see the surface is wet, drain off any excess water.

Lift up the seedlings by their small round seed leaves, which will appear before any other leaves.

6 Keep the seeds moist at all times, but never allow the compost to become waterlogged. When the seedlings appear, remove the plastic lids to prevent fungal diseases. When the seedlings have a few sets of leaves, transplant them to small pots of seed or multi-purpose compost. Use a fork to scoop them out.

7 Seedlings such as mizuna (above) can initially be potted up close together to grow on. Set 3–4 seedlings in 9cm (3½in) pots, taking care to gently firm the compost around them. Plant them so the lower stems are covered with compost.

8 Keep the pots of seedlings well watered and let them grow for a few weeks in a bright area until they are ready to harvest. If you want your crops to grow into mature plants, repot them again into a larger container and continue to grow on.

Pot method

You can sow seeds directly into 9cm (3½in) plastic pots filled with seed compost to save you transplanting large numbers of young seedlings later on. This is also best for planting large seeds, such as cucumbers, or where you just want to grow a few plants, such as peppers and tomatoes.

Sow
Sow 1–3 seeds per pot and cover them with the appropriate depth of compost or vermiculite as described on the pack. Label the pots.

Transplant
If more than one seed germinates, transplant the others into their own container filled with multi-purpose compost (steps 6–7, left), and move them into larger pots as they grow.

Pruning, training, & pollinating fruit crops

Cutting back the growing tip stimulates more side stems to form, resulting in a bushier, more productive plant

To keep your fruit trees **productive** you may need to **trim their stems** or cut out **old growth** from time to time. Follow these guidelines for the **best results** when pruning and training your plants.

Why prune?

There are several good reasons to prune a woody-stemmed plant such as a fruit tree. The first is to remove any dead or diseased growth, which should be cut out as soon as you see it. Pruning also rejuvenates the plant and encourages it to throw out new stems. If you remove the tip of the main stem, the plant will then grow more side shoots and become bushier which, in the case of fruit trees, means more fruit too. You can also prune your plant to reduce any congested growth, give it a better shape, and to ensure that all the developing fruits receive sufficient light.

Only use sharp tools that will produce clean cuts, and prune just above a bud or leaf stem.

Remove stems
Cut the longer stems from fruit crops such as makrut lime trees to create an evenly balanced shape and stimulate the growth of more fruiting side stems.

How to prune

When pruning, use a sharp pair of secateurs and make a clean cut just above a leaf or stem bud, above a leaf stem, or at the juncture of a main and a side stem. You can also cut out whole stems close to the base of the plant. Use a pruning saw or loppers for stems that are wider than a pencil and wear leather gloves when using this type of cutting tool. More specific pruning instructions are given for individual plants in Chapter 5.

Removing the top bud encourages more side stems to grow.

Cut just above a leaf bud or stem, or above a side stem.

Keep plants healthy
Remove old, diseased, or any wayward stems that may affect the plant's health, or spoil its shape, at the base.

Training

Some fruit trees, such as figs, can be trained into vase-like shapes, which not only look great but will produce more fruits, as each stem is evenly spaced to allow maximum light onto the branches. Training trees is best undertaken when the plants are young and their stems are flexible. As new growth emerges on the plant in spring, remove any stems that are spoiling the shape or crossing each other, as well as any suckers at the plant's base. Attach one end of a length of twine to a young stem at the edge of the plant and wrap the other end around a large pebble. Repeat with other stems. The pebbles will gradually pull the stems down gently to create a vase shape. Leave the stones in place for a season or two until the fig wood hardens. When you cut the stems free they should remain in that position. Continue to prune the plant annually, as described on p109.

Ensure the twine does not cut into the stems when tied on.

Training a fig to grow horizontal arms
In spring, tie the outer stems of a fig tree to pebbles with soft twine to coax them to grow horizontally and form an open vase-like shape.

Pollination

The key to fruit production is in a plant's flowers. Most flowers have the potential to produce a fruit or seedhead, but many need to be pollinated to fulfil their potential. Use the techniques below to encourage effective pollination for a bumper crop. Some plants, such as Cape gooseberries (physalis) and figs, are self-pollinating, meaning the pollen is transferred to the stigma (female organ) of the same flower, so the fruits will form without any help from you.

After fertilization, the flowers become the fruits.

Cucamelon flower with emerging fruit

Using a paintbrush

The crops below require the pollen from one flower to be transferred to the stigma of another flower. Insects do this job outdoors, but you need to perform the task for plants growing indoors.

- **citrus fruits**
- **strawberries**
- **pineapple guava**
- **cucamelons**
- **cucumbers**
- **aubergines**
- **peaches**
- **nectarines**

Use a clean, soft paintbrush to gently dust each flower, going from bloom to bloom to ensure all the pollen is transferred. Do this every day or two once the flowers appear to ensure they are all pollinated.

Lemons and other citrus fruits will need to be pollinated by hand.

Dusting a citrus flower

Shaking or spraying

Even if you are growing self-pollinating plants, you can encourage more fruits to form by gently shaking their stems to help distribute their pollen, or spray their flowers with a water mister a few times a week. Try these techniques with the following crops:

- **Cape gooseberries**
- **tomatoes**
- **sweet & chilli peppers**

Misting a sweet pepper flower

Common pests & diseases

One of the huge benefits of growing crops indoors is that you can more easily **protect your plants** from **flying** and **crawling insect pests** and some **airborne diseases**. However, a few problems may still occur, so be on your guard.

Pest-eating insects (biological controls) are useful in the garden, but in a home environment they may become a nuisance

Protecting your plants

Your crops are less likely to suffer attacks from pests and diseases if they are healthy. Protect plants by cleaning all pots and containers with detergent and hot water before planting, and use fresh compost for each project - buying smaller bags of compost will ensure it doesn't sit around for long. Keep plants well watered (avoid waterlogging), and feed them regularly, but do not overfeed, which can also cause poor growth.

Keep watering
Water plants regularly to keep them healthy so they are better equipped to fight off diseases.

Deficiencies & disorders

Not all symptoms of poor health are due to pests and diseases. Some, such as wilting, may simply be caused by a lack of water, while others can be the result of nutrient deficiency. However, most problems are easily rectified.

Tomatoes with blossom end rot.

BLOSSOM END ROT
This occurs in tomatoes that are suffering from a calcium deficiency. It occurs when plants are not watered frequently, since calcium is taken up by the roots in a solution. Remove affected fruits, and water the plants well.

NUTRIENT DEFICIENCY
Leaves that look pale and yellow between their veins is often a sign that the plant is suffering from an iron or nitrogen deficiency. Apply a liquid fertilizer for leafy crops - or, in the case of citrus fruits, for acid-loving crops - which should resolve the discoloration.

SPLIT FRUITS
Tomatoes and peppers are susceptible to splitting if the plants are not watered consistently, although they will still be edible. Try to keep the compost moist at all times, and avoid overwatering or allowing plants to dry out.

Identifying pests & diseases

Many people like to grow their own fruit and vegetables without using chemicals or pesticides. If you want to do this, check your plants regularly for any signs of pests and diseases, as they can usually be kept in check if caught early.

GREY MOULD
This is a common disease of soft fruits and vegetables that are grown in humid indoor conditions and results in a furry grey mould on buds, leaves, flowers, or fruit. To prevent it, remove dead or dying leaves, flowers, and fruits promptly, and increase the ventilation around plants by opening windows or using a fan. Do not overcrowd plants, as this also raises the humidity.

MEALYBUG
These little sap-feeding pests attack a range of edible plants such as citrus and peaches, reducing their vigour. They look like tiny flattened woodlice, and excrete a fluffy white wax and sticky substance, which may become infected by sooty moulds. Remove and discard affected plant parts. There are biological controls, but they are not always appropriate to a home environment.

DOWNY MILDEW
Lettuces and some flowers may be attacked by this fungal disease, which causes white, grey, or purple mould on the undersides of the leaves. Downy mildew is an airborne disease and affects plants growing in wet compost. Remove and discard any affected parts, ensure the compost is not waterlogged, avoid watering the leaves, and increase the air circulation in the room.

WHITEFLY
A common sap-feeding pest that weakens many crop plants, these tiny flies also excrete a sticky substance (honeydew), which then encourages black sooty moulds to develop. Hang sticky yellow sheets among your plants to trap the flies, or use an insecticide that is safe for crops. Setting the plants on a balcony may help too, as beneficial predators can then eat the flies.

Destroy adult vine weevils whenever you see them.

VINE WEEVIL
Often brought in on crop plants as young adults, the grubs of these pests do the most damage, eating entire root systems and causing plants to suddenly collapse. Check all new plants you buy and pick off and destroy the slow-moving, 9mm- (about $^{3}/_{8}$in-) long adults. The only effective controls are biological methods, which may not be appropriate for your home.

SLUGS & SNAILS
These molluscs tend not to enter a house, but they will scale walls to get to crops on windowsills and balconies, and may be present in the compost of bought edible plants. Look under pots during the day and dispatch any pests you find hiding there. You can also try fixing a band of copper tape around an outside windowbox – the copper gives them a slight electrical shock, which deters them.

Preserving your harvests

Although growing your own crops indoors rarely results in a glut and you will probably eat most of your produce fresh from the plant, these **recipes and ideas** offer you **easy ways to enjoy** some of your crops long after the **harvest period is over**.

To air-dry chillies, wrap strong thread around each stem and hang them up.

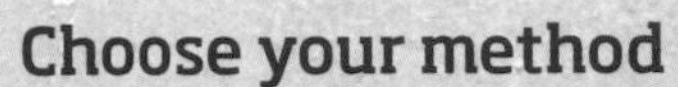

Choose your method

These effective preserving methods will extend the life of your produce, with all their delicious flavours and colours, for several months. For successful preservation, ensure your kitchen surfaces and equipment are absolutely clean.

Cooking

You can turn most of the fruits, root crops (such as beetroot), and fruiting vegetables in this book into chutneys and jams. Look online for simple jam recipes – most require equal amounts of fruit and jam sugar, although some soft-set jams require less sugar – and boil together to reach a setting point. Ensure that you carefully sterilize all jars and lids before potting up (see chutney recipe, opposite), and seal the jars properly.

Freezing

An effective preservation method, freezing is quick and convenient (see recipe, right). Freeze herbs and flowers as ice cubes – you can then add herb cubes to a recipe, or drop a flower ice cube into a drink. Fill an ice tray with chopped herbs and add approximately 1 tbsp of water to each module (to reach the rim of the tray) and freeze. For flowers, add one bloom to each module and fill with water. Use within 2 months.

Drying

Leave chillies on a sunny windowsill or hang in a warm, dry, airy place for 2 weeks or so until shrivelled. To air-dry tomatoes in a sunny spot indoors in summer, slice in half, remove the seeds, brush with olive oil, and leave, covered with muslin, on a wire tray for 2–4 days – or oven-dry them instead in a low oven at 120°C (250°F) for 2–3 hours. To store, place in sterilized jars (top right), cover with olive oil, and seal.

Jam wrinkles when it reaches the setting point.

Cooking jam

To test if your jam is ready, place a spoonful on a cold plate and leave to cool for a few minutes. Push your finger through the jam. If it wrinkles, it has set and is ready to be potted up.

Preserving herbs

If you have lots of herbs to preserve, follow the method above to make herb ice cubes, then transfer to a plastic freezer bag, label with the date, and return to the freezer until needed.

Dry the tomato halves on wire racks.

Oven-drying tomatoes

Score a cross shape in the centre of each halved tomato with a sharp knife to expose more of its flesh, sprinkle with a little salt, and place face down on the wire rack before oven-drying.

Freezer pickles

This recipe is quick and easy to make, and retains the crunchy bite of fresh cucumbers. Try the pickles in salads, sandwiches, as a relish with barbecued food, or as a condiment for savoury dishes. They will keep well in the freezer for up to six months. To use, thaw overnight in the fridge and consume within a week.

Ingredients

2 large cucumbers, thinly sliced
1 medium onion or 2 shallots, very thinly sliced
2 tsp sea salt
approx 120ml (4fl oz) cider or wine vinegar
approx 30-60g (1-2oz) caster sugar
¼ tsp celery or dill seeds
¼ tsp ground turmeric
1 tsp wholegrain mustard seeds
¼ tsp chilli flakes (optional)

1 Place the sliced cucumbers and onion or shallots in a large bowl, and sprinkle with salt. Mix well, and leave for 2 hours to draw out the moisture from the vegetables.

2 Transfer the salted vegetables to a colander and rinse under cold water. Drain well, pressing down on them lightly to squeeze out more moisture; then tip into a clean, dry bowl.

3 Mix the vinegar and sugar to taste, stirring well to ensure the granules dissolve, and then add the spices. Pour over the vegetables, mix well, cover, and store overnight in the fridge.

4 Transfer to plastic freezer pots, leaving a gap of 1cm (½in) at the top of each container. Seal, label with the date, and freeze for up to 6 months.

Tomato, red pepper, & chilli chutney

Red – and green – tomatoes are a fantastic base for a delicious chutney that will keep for up to 9 months in sterilized jars. To sterilize jars properly, either put both the jars and lids through a hot dishwasher cycle timed to be finished when the chutney is ready to be potted up, or wash them in hot water, drain upside down, and put in a cool oven (140°C/275°F/Gas 1) for about 15 minutes.

Ingredients

2 red peppers (skinned)
700g (1lb 8oz) ripe tomatoes (skinned and deseeded)
1 onion, roughly chopped
1-2 fresh red chillies (optional)
225g (8oz) granulated sugar
300ml (10fl oz) white wine vinegar

1 To remove the skins of the pepper easily, roast them in an oven at 200°C (400°F/Gas 6). Place the peppers on a baking tray and cook for up to 30 minutes until they are slightly charred. Remove from the oven, place in a plastic bag, and leave to cool. Pull off the stalks, peel off the skin, deseed, and chop roughly.

2 To skin the tomatoes, plunge them in boiling water for 1 minute and then peel and deseed them.

3 Put the tomato flesh, red peppers, onion, and chilli in a food processor and blitz briefly until the ingredients are all chopped but not mushy – or chop them well by hand. Transfer the mixture to a large, heavy-based, stainless steel saucepan or preserving pan and add the sugar and vinegar.

4 Cook on a low heat, stirring continuously using a wooden spoon until the sugar dissolves. Turn up the heat, bring to a boil, then reduce to a simmer and cook for approximately 1-1½ hours, stirring the mixture occasionally, until it thickens and turns jammy. Keep an eye on the heat – you may need to increase the heat slightly near the end of the cooking time – and stir continuously at this point so the chutney doesn't catch on the bottom of the pan.

5 Transfer to warm sterilized jars using a ladle, ensuring there are no air gaps in the potted mixture. Cover each pot with a waxed paper disc, seal, and label. Store in a cool, dark place for 1 month to allow the flavours to mature. Refrigerate after opening.

Useful resources

PLANTS & SEEDS

Aylett Nurseries Ltd
Suppliers of a wide range of indoor edible plants and seeds, and sundries
North Orbital Road, St Albans,
Hertfordshire, AL2 1DH
01727 822255
www.aylettnurseries.co.uk

Crocus
Suppliers of a wide range of indoor edible plants and seeds
Nursery Court, London Road,
Windlesham, Surrey GU20 6LQ
01344 578000
www.crocus.co.uk

Edible Ornamentals
Specialist supplier of chilli plants and seeds
Cherwood Nursery, Blue Bells,
Chawston, Bedford MK44 3BL
01480 405663
www.edibleornamentals.co.uk

Espresso Mushroom Company
UK supplier of simple-to-use, grow-your-own oyster mushroom kits
www.espressomushroom.com

Finchley Nurseries Ltd
For a wide range of mainly homegrown fruit and vegetable plants and seeds, and sundries
Burton Hole Lane, Mill Hill,
London NW7 1AS
020 8959 2124
www.finchleynurseries.net

Hooks Green Herbs
Specialists in culinary, medicinal and scented herb plants and seeds
07977 883810
www.hooksgreenherbs.com

Pomona Fruits
Specialists in fruit trees and plants
01255 440410
www.pomonafruits.co.uk

Paramount Plants & Gardens
Suppliers of fig trees and exotic fruit plants
131 Theobalds Park Road,
Crews Hill, Enfield,
London EN2 9BH
020 8367 8809
www.paramountplants.co.uk

Sea Spring Seeds
Specialist supplier of chilli plants and vegetable seeds
Sea Spring Farm, West
Bexington, Dorchester,
Dorset DT2 9DD
01308 897898
www.seaspringseeds.co.uk

Seeds of Italy
Specialists in vegetable seeds, and fruit and herb plants from Italy
Paolo Arrigo, Phoenix
Business Centre, Unit D2,
Rosslyn Crescent, Harrow,
Middlesex HA1 2SP
0208 427 5020
www.seedsofitaly.com

South Devon Chilli Farm
Specialist supplier of chilli plants and seeds
Wigford Cross, Loddiswell,
Devon TQ7 4DX
Tel: 01548 550782
www.southdevonchillifarm.co.uk

Suttons Seeds
Suppliers of a wide range of fruit and vegetable seeds and plants
Woodview Road, Paignton,
Devon TQ4 7NG
0844 3262200
www.suttons.co.uk

Tom Smith Plants
Specialist supplier of soft fruit bushes and trees
07543 661504
www.tomsmithplants.com

Thompson & Morgan
Suppliers of a wide range of fruit and vegetable seeds and plants
Poplar Lane, Ipswich,
Suffolk IP8 3BU
0844 5731818
www.thompson-morgan.com

Squires Garden Centres
Suppliers of a wide range of edible plants and seeds, and sundries
01252 356860
www.squiresgardencentres.co.uk

Victoriana Nursery Gardens
Specialist supplier of fruit trees and herbs, vegetable plants and seeds
Buck Street, Challock, Ashford,
Kent TN25 4DG
01233 740529
www.victoriananursery.co.uk

CONTAINERS & SUNDRIES

Conpot
Handmade concrete pots
www.conpot.co.uk

elho
For a wide range of lightweight indoor pots for edibles
+31 (0)13 515 78 00
www.elho.com

GroWell
Suppliers of grow lights and hydroponics units for domestic use
0333 0032296
www.growell.co.uk

Habitat
For a wide range of indoor containers
0344 4994686
www.habitat.co.uk

Ikea
For a wide range of indoor containers and easy-to-use hydroponics units
020 36450000
www.ikea.com

CHARITIES

The Shaw Trust Horticultural Project
Charity supporting people marginalized by society; supplying homegrown vegetable and fruit plants at open days and fairs
0345 2349675
www.shaw-trust.org.uk

Index

Entries in italics refer to general (plant group) and species, for example *Allium* and *Capsicum*, which are abbreviated if there is more than one variety.

A

Acca sellowiana 192–93
adzuki beansprouts in jars 83
aggregates 201
alfalfa sprouts in jars 83
all-purpose compost 200
Allium species 104–05
  A. cepa 'Apache' 105
  A. c. 'White Lisbon' 105
  A. fistulosum 'Performer' 105
  A. schoenoprasum 105
  A. tuberosum 105
Aloysia citrodora 49
amaranth, microgreen seeds 88, 89
Anise hyssop 62
Asian-style leafy crops 99
aubergines 136–37
  aftercare 136
  'Black Beauty' 137
  cook's tips 137
  harvesting 137
  height of growth 26, 133
  how to grow 136
  light & heat 19, 26, 136
  'Pinstripe' 137
  pollination 207
  'Raja' 137
  storage and preserving 137
  Thai aubergines 137
  varieties 137
  watering 136
  when to buy 136
  when to plant 136, 198, 199
  when to sow 136, 198
  where to grow 18, 19, 26

B

bark, edible orchids mounted onto 52–55
basil 24, 46–47
  aftercare 46
  and bees 43
  bush basil 47, 127
  compost to plant in 46
  cook's tips 47
  'Dark opal' 47
  harvesting 46, 199
  how to grow 69, 91
  lemon basil 47
  light & heat 46
  microgreen seeds 88, 89
  scented geranium & herb windowbox 42–45
  spice basil 47
  sweet basil 47
  Thai basil 44–45, 47
  varieties 47
  watering 46
  when to buy 46
  when to sow 46, 198, 199
  when to plant 198, 199
baskets 30
beans, sprouts in jars 80–81
bees 43
beetroot
  'Barbietola di Chioggia' 107
  'Boltardy' 107
  'Burpee's Golden' 107
  choosing 107
  cook's tips 89, 106
  growing beetroot from plugs 109
  harvesting 25
  how to grow 109
  microgreen seeds 88, 89
  pots of tasty roots 106–09
  when to plant 198, 199
  when to sow 25, 198
  where to grow 106
bellis daisy 56
  harvesting 198
  when to plant 198
blossom end rot 208
bowls (as planters) 127
bright sunlight zones 16, 18–19
broccoli
  microgreens 78
  sprouts in jars 82
buckets 69
bulbs, when to plant 198–99

C

calamondin oranges 180–83, 184
  compost 201
  feeding 180, 182
  harvesting 26, 198
  overwintering 26
  repotting 182–83
  watering 180
  when to plant 198, 199
Cape gooseberries 26, 194–95
  aftercare 194
  best growing zones for 167
  cook's tips 195
  flowers 194
  growing on windowsills 166
  harvesting 194
  how to grow 194
  light & heat 194
  pollination 194, 207
  watering 194, 195
  when to buy 194
  when to plant 198, 199
Capsicum 130–31
  C. annuum 131, 162–63
  C. a. 'Cayenne' 131
  C. a. 'Chilly Chili' 131
  C. a. 'Jalapeno' 131
  C. a. 'Loco' 131
  C. baccatum 131
  C. b. 'Aji Amarillo' 131
  C. b. 'Lemon Drop' 131
  C. chinense 131
  C. c. 'Dorset Naga' 131
carnations 57
carrot root fly 112
carrots 116–17
  aftercare 116
  carrot root fly 112
  choosing containers for 29, 112, 116
  cook's tips 117
  drainage 112
  feeding 115, 116
  germination 115
  growing time 112, 115
  harvesting 116, 199
  how to grow 115, 116
  light & heat 116
  'Nantes' 117
  pesticides 78
  pots of crunchy carrots 112–15
  'Purple Haze' 117
  'Royal Chantenay' 117
  'St Valery' 117
  thinning out 115
  varieties 25, 112, 117
  watering 115, 116
  when to buy 116
  when to plant 198, 199
  when to sow 25, 116, 198, 199
  where to grow 17, 112
  'White Satin' 117
centre of a room zone
  and fruit 167
  and fruiting vegetables 125
  and herbs & flowers 35
  partially sunlit zones 16, 20, 21
  and sprouts, leaves & roots 79
  suitable plants for 20
chamomile tea 49
chickpea sprouts in jars 83
chilli peppers 26, 130–31
  aftercare 130
  Aji 131
  'Aji Amarillo' 131
  'Cayenne' 131
  chilli & herb ball 126–29
  chilli 'Apache' 127
  chilli 'Prairie Fire' 127
  'Chilly Chili' 131
  choosing containers for 29

companion plants 133, 177
compost to use 130
cook's tips 131, 211
'Dorset Naga' 131
drying 210
feeding 128, 130
grow lights 130
growing in cool zones 23
growing on windowsills 125
Habanero types 131
harvesting 130
heat ratings 130
how to grow 130
'Jalapeno' 131
'Lemon Drop' 131
light & heat 130
'Loco' 131
Mediterranean mix 133
pollination 207
tomato, red pepper, and chilli chutney 211
varieties 127, 131
watering 126, 130
when to buy 130
when to plant 198, 199
when to sow 130, 198
where to grow 23, 125

chives 24, 104–05
cook's tips 105
flowers 59
garden chives 105
garlic chives 105
harvesting 37, 198, 199
how to grow 104
light requirements 37
varieties 105
when to plant 198, 199
when to sow 198, 199

chop suey 99

chutney 210
tomato, red pepper, and chilli chutney 211

x *Citrofortunella microcarpa* 184

citrus fruit 166
feeding 180
mealybug 209
overwintering citrus trees 17, 22, 167
pollination 207
watering 180
see also lemons; limes; oranges, *etc*

Citrus
C. × *aurantiifolia* 179
C. hystrix 179
C. japonica 184
C. × *latifolia* 179
C. × *meyeri* 179
C. reticulata 184
C. sinensis 184

cocktails
cocktail herbs & fruits 62–65
mint & cucamelon Pimm's 65
strawberry Martini 65

coconut husks 203

colanders
growing salad leaves in 101
tiny tomatoes in a colander 138–41

compost 208
choosing the right compost 200–01
multi-purpose 45
testing moisture 202

containers
alternative containers 69
bespoke containers on wheels 150–53
bowls as baskets 127
choosing 28–29, 107
cleaning 208
galvanized tubs 132
for root vegetables 112
size 29
types of 30–31

cool zones 22–23
cool, south-facing rooms 16, 17, 22
and fruit 23, 167
and fruiting vegetables 23, 125
and herbs & flowers 23, 35
outside windowsills 16, 17, 22
and sprouts, leaves & roots 23, 79
suitable plants for 22

copper tape 43, 209

coriander 91
microgreen seeds 88

Cos lettuce 97

cowslips 57

crates
growing cucamelons in hanging crates 156–59
growing cucumbers on wheels 148–53

cucamelons 26
cocktail herbs & fruits 62–65
cook's tips 63, 157
ensuring even growth 159
feeding 159
frost 22
growing in hanging crates 156–59
growing outside 22, 125
growing tips 157, 159
light requirements 157
mint & cucamelon Pimm's 65
pollinating 158, 159, 207
watering 159
when to plant 198, 199
when to sow 198
where to grow 22, 125

cucumbers 26, 154–55
aftercare 154
'Bush Champion' 155
'Carmen' 155
cook's tips 155, 211
'Cucino' 155
cucumbers on wheels 148–53
'Delizia' 155
feeding 154
freezer pickles 211
growing temperature 152, 154
harvesting 149, 153, 154
health benefits 124
how to grow 154, 204
light requirements 149, 153, 154
pinching out 153
pollination 149, 207
space requirements 124
supporting 151, 153, 154
varieties 149, 155
watering 154
when to buy 154
when to plant 154, 198, 199
when to sow 154, 198
where to grow 19

Cucumis sativus 154–55

curry leaves, grow your own 176–77

cutting compost 200

D

daikon radish 111

damping-off disease 204

dark corners 16
fruit 167
fruiting vegetables 125
herbs & flowers 35
sprouts, leaves & roots 79
suitable plants for 20

deadheading 45

dendrobiums
aftercare 55
'Berry Oda' 53
cook's tips 24, 53, 57
edible orchids mounted onto bark 52–55
feeding 55
harvesting 198, 199
nobile type 53
Phalaenopsis type 53
watering 54, 55
when to plant 198, 199

Dianthus species 57

diseases 208–09
blossom end rot 208
damping-off disease 204
downy mildew 202, 209
grey mould 202, 209
importance of drainage 29
mildew 59, 209
protecting against fungal diseases 22, 205

pruning to prevent 206
and watering 202
drainage
and choosing containers 28, 29
herbs & flowers 38, 39
horticultural gravel & grit 201
and watering 202
windowboxes 44
drying produce 210

E

east-facing windows
and fruit 167
and fruiting vegetables 19, 125
and herbs & flowers 35
and sprouts, leaves & roots 79
suitable plants for 17, 18
enoki mushrooms 120
cook's tips 121
ericaceous compost 201

F

feeding 202-03
edible flowers 56, 58
feeding fruit trees 203
fertilizers for long-term crops 203
fruiting vegetables 133, 135
herbs & flowers 39, 40, 51
nutrient deficiency 208
nutrients required 203
preparing fertilizer 203
windowboxes 45
see also individual fruit and vegetables
feijoas (pineapple guava) 27, 166, 192-93
aftercare 192
cook's tips 193
drainage 192
flowers 27
harvesting 192
how to grow 192
light & heat 27, 192
pollination 192, 207
watering 192
when to buy 192
when to plant 198, 199
fenugreek, microgreen seeds 88, 89
fertilizers 202-03
edible flowers 56, 58
feeding fruit trees 203
fertilizers for long-term crops 203
fruiting vegetables 133, 135
herbs & flowers 39, 40, 51
nutrient deficiency 208
nutrients required 203
preparing fertilizer 203
windowboxes 45
see also individual fruit and vegetables
feverfew 49
fibreglass containers 31
Ficus carica 186-89
figs 188-89
'Brown Turkey' 187
'Brunswick' 187
choosing containers for 29
feeding 203
how to grow 186-87
light requirements 19, 26
overwintering 22, 26, 167
pruning 188, 189
training 207
varieties 187
'Violette de Sollies' 187
watering 189
when to plant 198, 199
Flammulina velutipes 120
flowers, edible 34, 56-57
aftercare 39, 56
bellis daisy 56, 198
best zones for 35
carnations 57
choosing containers for 29
cook's tips 24, 57
edible flower ladder 58-59
edible orchids mounted onto bark 52-55
feeding 56, 58
freezing 210
fruit & flower windowbox 174-75
geraniums 34, 42-45
growing in pots 38-39
harvesting 56
herbs & edible flowers in pots for a windowsill 36
how to grow 56
indoor varieties 56-57
lavender 34, 57, 59, 198, 199
light & heat 35, 56
orchids 24, 52-55, 57, 198, 199
pansies 56, 57, 59
primroses 34, 57, 59, 198
scented geranium & herb windowbox 42-45
tulips 24, 56, 57, 198, 199
violas 24, 34, 36, 39, 56, 57, 59, 198, 199
watering 56, 58, 59
when to buy 56
when to plant 198, 199
when to sow 198, 199
where to grow 35
Fragaria species 172-73
F. × *ananassa* 'Albion' 173
F. × *a.* 'Frau Mieze Schindler' 173
F. × *a.* 'Honeoye' 173
F. × *a.* 'Mara des Bois' 173
F. × *a.* 'Snow White' 173
F. vesca 173
freezer pickles 211
freezing produce 210
fruit 26-27, 164-95
best growing zones for 167
cocktail herbs & fruits 62-65
feeding fruit trees 203
fruit & flower windowbox 174-75
pruning 206
training 207
see also individual types of fruit
fruiting vegetables 26, 122-63
best growing zones for 125
feeding 133, 135
see also individual types of fruiting vegetables
fungal diseases 209
damping-off disease 204
downy mildew 202, 209
grey mould 202, 209
protecting against 22, 29, 205
and watering 202

G

garlic, tangy shoots 102-03
garlic greens
harvesting 25, 199
how to grow 78
when to plant 198, 199
when to sow 198
geraniums 34
'Orange Fizz' 44
scented geranium 43
scented geranium & herb windowbox 42-45
germination 204-05
glass chips 201
glasses 69
tangy garlic shoots 102-03
glazed clay pots 30
gravel 39, 201
'Green Batavian' lettuce 97
'Green Oak Leaf' lettuce 97
greenhouses, mini 90-93
grey mould 202, 209
grow lights
hydroponics 203
in mini greenhouses 90, 91, 92-95
raising lettuce from seed 94-95
using in partially sunlit zones 20, 21
growing zones 16-23, 25
best for fruit 167
best for fruiting vegetables 125
best for herbs & flowers 35
best for sprouts, leaves & roots 79

H

hanging containers and shelves 31
- chilli & herb ball 126–29
- grow your own herbal teas 48–51
- growing cucamelons in hanging crates 156–59
- herbs in hanging jars 68–71
- tiny tomatoes in a colander 138–41

harvesting produce 198–99
- preserving your harvests 210–11
- *see also individual fruit and vegetables*

herbs 24, 32–51, 60–75
- aftercare 39
- best growing zones 16, 17, 19, 21, 23, 35
- chilli & herb ball 126–29
- choosing containers for 29
- cocktail herbs & fruits 62–65
- feeding 51
- freezing 210
- grow herbs & flowers in pots 38–39
- grow lights 91
- grow your own herbal teas 48–51
- growing in cool zones 22, 23
- growing lemongrass from shop-bought stems 60–61
- growing outside 16
- herbs in hanging jars 68–71
- picking 48
- scented geranium & herb windowbox 42–45
- watering 51, 70, 126
- where to grow 35
- *see also individual types of herb*

horticultural gravel & grit 201
hydroponics 203
hyssop, cocktail herbs & fruits 62–65

I

ice bucket 64

J

jams 210
jars
- herbs in hanging jars 68–71
- sprouts in jars 80–81

John Innes compost 200

K

kaffir lime plant 176–77
- pruning 206

kale, microgreen seeds 88, 89
king oyster mushrooms 121
kumquats 180–83
- compost 201
- cook's tips 184
- harvesting 27, 180, 198
- overwintering 27
- repotting 182–83
- when to plant 198, 199

L

Lactuca sativa 96–97
ladders, edible flower 58–59
Lavandula species 57
lavender
- cook's tips 57, 59
- health benefits of 34
- how to grow 59
- when to plant 198, 199

leafy vegetables
- growing in bright sunlit zones 18, 19
- growing in cool zones 22
- growing in partially sunlit zones 16, 17, 22
- when to plant 198, 199
- when to sow 198, 199
- *see also individual types of vegetable*

lemon verbena 49
- harvesting 198, 199
- lemon verbena tea 49
- when to plant 198, 199

lemongrass
- caring for & harvesting 24, 61
- growing from shop-bought stems 60–61

lemons 178–79
- aftercare 178
- choosing pots 178
- compost 178, 201
- cook's tips 179
- feeding 178
- harvesting 179, 198
- how to grow 178
- light requirements 27, 178
- Meyer lemon 179
- overwintering 27, 166, 178
- preserving & storing 179
- varieties 178
- watering 178
- when to buy 178
- when to plant 198, 199

lentils, sprouts in jars 82
Lentinula edodes 120
lettuce
- aftercare 96
- choosing containers for 29, 91
- cook's tips 97
- Cos 97
- downy mildew 202, 209
- feeding 96
- 'Green Batavian' 97
- 'Green Oak Leaf' 97
- harvesting 198, 199
- how to grow 96, 99
- light requirements 23, 25, 99
- 'Little Gem' 97
- 'Lollo Rossa' 97
- overwintering 23
- 'Red Oak Leaf' 97
- sowing from seed 94–95, 204
- table-top spicy leaves 98–101
- varieties 97
- watering 96
- when to buy 96
- when to plant 96, 198, 199
- when to sow 23, 96, 198, 199
- where to grow 20, 23, 25, 79

lighting
- bright sunlight zones 16, 18–19
- grow lights 20, 21, 90–95, 203
- hydroponics 203
- partially sunlit zones 20–21
- transforming shelves into mini greenhouses 90–95
- turning pots to aid growth 37

limes 178–79
- aftercare 178
- choosing containers 178
- compost 178, 201
- cook's tips 179
- feeding 178
- harvesting 179, 198
- how to grow 178
- Key lime 179
- light requirements 27, 178
- makrut (kaffir) lime 27, 176–77, 179
- overwintering 166, 178
- pruning 206
- storing 179
- Tahiti lime 179
- varieties 178
- watering 178
- when to buy 178
- when to plant 198, 199

'Little Gem' 97
loam-based compost 200
'Lollo Rossa' 97

M

makrut (kaffir) lime leaves 176–77, 179
- pruning 206

mandarin orange 27, 184
marigolds 34
- fruit & flower windowbox 174–75
- when to plant 198, 199
- when to sow 198, 199

marjoram 72, 73
Martini, strawberry 65
mealybug 209

Mediterranean mix 132–35
Mentha species 66–67
- *M.* × *piperita* 49, 66
- *M.* × *p. f. citrata* 'Basil' 66
- *M.* × *p. f. c.* 'Chocolate' 67
- *M.* × *p. f. c.* 'Lime' 67
- *M. suaveolens* 67
- *M. s.* 'Pineapple' 67

metal containers 31
mibuna 25, 99
- cook's tips 25, 99
- harvesting 198, 199
- when to plant 198, 199
- when to sow 198, 198

microgreens 25, 88–89
- batch-sowing 87
- choosing containers for 29, 87
- cook's tips 84, 89
- growing time 77, 78, 84
- harvesting 84, 87, 198, 199
- health benefits of 84
- how to grow 87, 88, 91
- light requirements 87
- microgreens in muffin cases 84–87
- varieties 89
- watering 87
- when to sow 198, 199

mildew 59
- downy mildew 202, 209

mint 66–67
- aftercare 66
- apple mint 67
- basil mint 66
- chocolate mint 67
- choosing containers 66, 68, 69
- cocktail herbs & fruits 62–65
- cook's tips 63, 67
- feeding 66
- harvesting 24, 66, 198, 199
- health benefits of 34
- herbs in hanging jars 68–71
- how to grow 66
- Indian trailing mint 67
- light & heat 36, 66
- lime mint 67
- mint & cucamelon Pimm's 65
- mint tea 34, 49
- pineapple mint 67
- propagating 67
- varieties 67
- watering 66
- when to buy 198
- when to plant 198, 199

mirrors 20
mizuna 25
- containers 94
- cook's tips 25, 99
- harvesting 198, 199
- microgreen seeds 88, 89
- potting on seedlings 205
- table-top spicy leaves 98
- temperature requirements 99
- watering 99
- when to plant 198, 199
- when to sow 198, 199

mooli 111
mould, grey 202, 209
muffin cases, microgreens in 84–87
mulches 201
multi-purpose compost 200
mung bean sprouts in jars 80–81, 83
mushrooms
- aftercare 120
- cook's tips 121
- enoki mushrooms 120
- growing oyster mushrooms in 14 days 118–19
- harvesting 25, 119, 120, 199
- how to grow 120
- king oyster mushrooms 121
- light & heat 120
- mushroom kits 25, 118–19, 120
- oyster mushrooms 121
- shiitake mushrooms 120
- varieties 120–21
- watering 120
- when to buy 120
- where to grow 20

mustard, microgreen seeds 88, 89

N

nasturtiums
- fruit & flower windowbox 174–75
- harvesting 199
- when to plant 198, 199
- when to sow 198

nectarines 190–91
- aftercare 191
- best growing zones for 167
- cook's tips 191
- feeding 27
- harvesting 191
- how to grow 190–91
- light & heat 166, 190
- 'Lord Napier' 191
- pollination 27, 166, 207
- varieties 191
- watering 190
- when to buy 190
- when to plant 198, 199
- where to grow 22

nitrogen 203, 208
north-facing rooms 20
nutrient deficiency 208

O

Ocimum basilicum 46–47
- *O. basilicum* 'Dark Opal' 47
- *O. b.* 'Spice' 47
- *O. b.* var. *thyrsiflorum* 47
- *O.* × *citriodorum* 47
- *O. minimum* 'Bush' 47

ollas 141
oranges 184–85
- aftercare 184
- compost 201
- cook's tips 185
- feeding 180, 182, 184
- harvesting 184, 198
- how to grow 27, 184
- light & heat 27, 184, 185
- mandarin orange 27, 184
- oranges in pots for a sunny room 180–83
- overwintering 27, 166
- repotting 182–83
- sweet orange 184
- varieties 184
- watering 180, 184
- when to buy 184
- when to plant 198, 199
- *see also* calamondin oranges; kumquats

orchids
- 'Berry Oda' 53
- caring for 55
- cook's tips 24, 57
- edible orchids mounted onto bark 52–55
- feeding 55
- harvesting 198, 199
- nobile type 53
- Phalaenopsis type 53
- watering 54, 55
- when to plant 198, 199

oregano 24, 72–73
- aftercare 72
- choosing containers 72
- compost to use 72
- cook's tips 73
- golden oregano 73
- harvesting 72
- how to grow 72, 91
- light & heat 72
- sweet marjoram 73
- variegated oregano 73
- varieties 73
- watering 72
- when to buy 72
- when to plant 72

Origanum
- *O. majorana* 73
- *O. vulgare* 72–3
- *O. v.* 'Aureum' 73
- *O. v.* 'County Cream' 73

oyster mushrooms 121
- cook's tips 121
- growing in 14 days 118–19
- harvesting 119

P

pak choi 25
cook's tips 99
harvesting 198, 199
watering 98
when to plant 198, 199
when to sow 198, 199
pansy (*see* viola) 59
cook's tips 56, 57
parsley 36, 72–73
aftercare 72
choosing containers 72
compost to use 72
cook's tips 73
curly-leaved parsley 73
flat-leaved parsley 73
harvesting 72, 198, 199
light & heat 24, 72
varieties 73
watering 72
when to buy 72
when to plant 198, 199
when to sow 198, 199
peaches 190–91
aftercare 191
'Avalon Pride' 191
best growing zones for 167
'Bonanza' 191
choosing containers 190
compost 190
cook's tips 191
feeding 203
harvesting 191
how to grow 190–91
light & heat 27, 166, 190
mealybug 209
overwintering 27
pollination 166, 207
varieties 191
watering 190
when to buy 190
when to plant 198, 199
where to grow 22
peppermint
cook's tips 63, 67
how to grow 49
peppermint tea 49, 66
peppers, sweet 26, 162–63
aftercare 162
'Boneta' 163
choosing containers for 29
compost to use 162
cook's tips 163, 211
feeding 162
growing in bright sunlit zones 18, 19, 22
growing outside 22
harvesting 161, 162, 199
health benefits 124
how to grow 162, 205
light & heat 18, 161, 162
'Lunchbox Mix' 162
'Luteus' 162
'Mohawk' 162
pollination 207
raising sweet peppers in colourful pots 160–61
split fruits 208
supporting 161
'Tequila' 162
'Thor' 162
tomato, red pepper, and chilli chutney 211
varieties 133, 162–63
watering 162, 208
when to buy 162
when to plant 198, 199
when to sow 198
where to grow 18, 19, 22, 125
perlite 201
pests 208–09
carrot root fly 112
mealybug 209
preventing 43
slugs and snails 209
vine weevils 209
whitefly 209
Petroselinum crispum 72–73
P. c. var. *neapolitanum* 73
phosphorous 203
Physalis peruviana 194–95
pickles, freezer 211
Pimm's, mint & cucamelon 65
pinching out
cucumbers 153
tomatoes 135
pineapple guava 27, 166, 192–93
aftercare 192
cook's tips 193
harvesting 192
how to grow 192
light & heat 27, 192
pollination 192, 207
watering 192
when to buy 192
when to plant 198, 199
pinks 57
planning your indoor edible garden 198–99
planters 30
plastic containers 31, 69
Pleurotus
P. eryngii 121
P. ostreatus 121
pollination
Cape gooseberries 194
cucamelons 158
insect pollination 22
peaches & nectarines 191
pineapple guava 192
strawberries 168, 174
techniques 134, 207
polyanthus 57
pot marigolds 34
fruit & flower windowbox 174–75
when to sow/plant 198, 199
potash 203
potassium 203
pots 30–31
alternative containers 69
choosing 28–29
cleaning 208
growing herbs & flowers in 38–39
pots of crunchy carrots 112–15
pots of tasty roots 106–09
raising sweet peppers in colourful pots 160–61
size of 29
potting up herbs & flowers 37
preserving fruit & vegetables 210–11
primroses 34, 57
cook's tips 57
drainage 59
harvesting 198
when to plant 198
Primula species 57
propagators 91, 205
pruning
figs 188, 189
tamarillo tree tomato 147
techniques 206
Prunus
P. persica 190–91
P. p. 'Avalon Pride' 191
P. p. 'Bonanza' 191
P. p. var. *nectarina* 'Lord Napier' 191
pumice stones 203

R

radishes 110–11
aftercare 110
'Amethyst' 111
'Cherry Belle' 107
choosing 107
choosing containers for 29
cook's tips 106, 111
'French Breakfast' 111
growing radishes from seed 25, 108, 91
harvesting 110, 199
how to grow 108, 110
'Kulata Cerna' 111
light & heat 110
microgreens 78, 88
mooli 110, 111
pots of tasty roots 106–09
'Scarlet Globe' 111
'Sparkler' 111
varieties 78, 111

watering 108, 110
when to buy 110
when to plant 110, 198, 199
when to sow 110, 198, 199
where to grow 106
'Zlata' 111
Raphanus sativus 110–11
'Red Oak Leaf' 97
resin containers 31
rocket, microgreen seeds 88
root vegetables
growing in cool zones 22
growing in partially sunlit zones 20, 21
pots of tasty roots 106–09
where to grow 20, 21, 22, 79
see also individual types of root vegetable
rosemary
care of 36, 74
compost to use 74
cook's tips 36, 75
feeding 74
growing herbs & flowers in pots 38–39
harvesting 24, 74, 198, 199
health benefits of 34
how to grow 74
light & heat 74
varieties 75
watering 74
when to buy 74
when to plant 198, 199
where to grow 23
Rosmarinus officinalis 74–75

S

sage 24
aftercare 74
blackcurrant sage 75
common sage 75
compost to use 74
containers to use 37
cook's tips 75
feeding 74
growing herbs & flowers in pots 38, 39
harvesting 74, 198, 199
health benefits of 34
herbs in hanging jars 68–71
how to grow 74
'Icterina' sage 75
light & heat 74
pineapple sage 68, 75
purple sage 75
'Tricolor' sage 75
varieties 75
watering 74
when to buy 74
when to plant 198, 199
where to grow 23, 37
salad leaves 78
aftercare 96
choosing containers for 29, 91
cook's tips 97
Cos lettuce 97
downy mildew 202, 209
feeding 96
'Green Batavian' lettuce 97
harvesting 198, 199
how to grow 96, 99
light & heat 23, 25, 96
'Little Gem' 97
'Lollo Rossa' 97
overwintering 23
'Red Oak Leaf' 97
sowing from seed 94–95, 204
table-top spicy leaves 98–101
varieties 97
watering 96
when to plant 96, 198, 199
when to sow 23, 96, 198, 199
where to grow 20, 23, 25, 79
Salvia
S. elegans 'Scarlet Pineapple' 75
S. microphylla var. *microphylla* 75
S. officinalis 74–75
S. o. 'Icterina' 75
S. o. 'Purpurascens' 75
S. o. 'Tricolor' 75
Satureja douglasii 67
Scoville Heat Units (SHU) 130
seashells 201
seed compost 200
seedlings, transplanting 205
seeds
sowing from seed 204–05
when to sow 198–99
shelves
mini greenhouse 90–93
suspended shelves for herbs 48–51
wild strawberry shelves 168–71
shiitake mushrooms 120
cook's tips 121
skylights
and fruit 167
and fruiting vegetables 125
growing lettuce beneath 95
and herbs & flowers 35
as source of bright sunlight 16, 17, 19
and sprouts, leaves & roots 79
suitable plants for growing beneath 18
slugs and snails 209
copper tape as deterrent 43, 209
soil-based compost 200
Solanum
S. betaceum 146
S. lycopersicum 142–43
S. melongena 136–37
sorrel
cook's tips 43
scented geranium & herb windowbox 42–45
watering 42
south-facing rooms 22
south-facing windows
and fruit 19, 167
and fruiting vegetables 19, 125
and herbs & flowers 35
as source of bright sunlight 16
and sprouts, leaves & roots 79
suitable plants for 18, 19
spearmint 63
spring onions 104–05
aftercare 104
'Apache' 105
cook's tips 105
flowers 104
harvesting 104, 199
how to grow 104
light & heat 25, 104
'Performer' 105
varieties 105
watering 104
when to buy 104
when to plant 104, 198, 199
when to sow 91, 104, 198, 199
'White Lisbon' 105
sprouts
aftercare 82
cook's tips 83
growing time 77
harvesting 82, 198, 199
health benefits 78
light & heat 82
sprouts in jars 25, 80–81, 82
storing 81
varieties 82–83
watering 82
when to buy 82
when to sow 198, 199
where to grow 20, 79
stevia
harvesting 198, 199
stevia tea 49
when to plant 198, 199
disclaimer 221
strawberries 172–73
aftercare 168, 172
'Albion' 173
alpine strawberries 16, 17
cocktail herbs & fruits 62–65
cook's tips 173
feeding 168, 172, 174
'Frau Mieze Schindler' 173
fruit & flower windowbox 174–75
growing in bright sunlit zones 17, 19, 27
growing outside 16, 22, 23

growing in partially lit zones 21, 167
harvesting 172, 199
'Honeoye' 173
how to grow 27, 168, 172
light & heat 27, 172
'Mara des Bois' 173
planting bare-root strawberry plants 173
pollination 166, 168, 174, 207
'Snow White' 173
sowing strawberry seeds 172
strawberry Martini 65
varieties 27, 63, 173
watering 170, 172
when to buy 172
when to plant 198, 199
where to grow 167
wild strawberries 21, 168–71, 173
wild strawberry shelves 168–71
sunflowers, microgreens in muffin cases 86–87
sunlight 16
bright sunlight zones 16, 18–19
partially sunlit zones 20–21
sweet Williams 57

T

table-top spicy leaves 98–101
tamarillo tree tomato 26, 146–47
aftercare 147
cook's tips 147
fruit 147
harvesting 147
how to grow 146
light & heat 26, 146
pruning 147
watering 146
Tanacetum parthenium 49
teas, grow your own herbal 48–51
temperature 22
terracotta pots 30
thyme 24
aftercare 40
alpine thyme 41
choosing containers 37
common thyme 40, 41
compost to use 40
cook's tips 41, 42
creeping red thyme 41
creeping thyme 43
encouraging new leaf growth 127
flowers 40
harvesting 24, 40, 198, 199
herbs in hanging jars 68–71
how to grow 40, 113
lemon thyme 41
light & heat 40, 91, 113
repotting 40
scented geranium & herb windowbox 42–45
size 37
'Silver Posie' thyme 41
varieties 41
watering 40
when to buy 40
when to plant 198, 199
wild thyme 41
Thymus
T. 'Coccineus Group' 41
T. pulegioides 'Archer's Gold' 41
T. serpyllum 41
T. 'Silver Posie' 41
T. vulgaris 40–41
T. 'Worfield Gardens' 41
tomatoes 142–43
'Balconi' 139
benefits of 124
'Black Cherry' 143
blossom end rot 208
bush tomatoes 20, 133, 138, 139
caring for 141, 142
choosing containers for 29, 142
cook's tips 143, 211
drying 210
feeding 141, 142
growing in bright sunlit zones 18, 19, 125
growing in cool zones 22, 23
growing in partially sunlit zones 20, 125
harvesting 142
how to grow 142
light & heat 142
Mediterranean mix 132–35
'Moneymaker' 143
'Olivade' 143
patio tomatoes 16, 17
pinching out 135
pollination 207
'Satyna' 143
size 142
sowing from seed 204, 205
split fruits 208
'Sungold' 143
tamarillo tree tomato 26, 146–47
'Tigerella' 143
tiny tomatoes in a colander 138–41
tomato, red pepper, and chilli chutney 211
tomato towers 144–45
'Totem' 142
Tumbling Tom' 139
varieties 26, 139, 142, 143
'Vilma' 143
watering 141, 142, 145, 208
when to sow 142, 198
when to plant 198, 199
training 207
transplanting seedlings 205
trellis
cucumber units 151
tomato towers 145
trolleys, cocktail herbs & fruits 62–65
tulips
cook's tips 56, 57
growing tips 24
harvesting 198, 199
when to plant 198

V

vegetables, fruiting 26, 124–25
see also fruiting vegetables
ventilation, increasing to encourage growth 40, 114, 135, 139
vermiculite 201, 204
vine weevils 209
violas
cook's tips 36, 56, 57
flowering time 24, 34, 59
harvesting 198, 199
how to grow 36, 39
when to plant 198, 199
when to sow 198, 199

W

walls 16, 17, 20
and fruit 167
and fruiting vegetables 125
and herbs & flowers 35
and sprouts, leaves & roots 20, 21, 79
suitable plants for 20, 21
watering 202–03
herbs 39, 51, 70, 126
microgreens 87
and preventing diseases 208
seedlings 205
self-watering planters 28
sprouts 82
see also individual fruit and vegetables
west-facing windows
and fruit 18, 19, 167
and fruiting vegetables 18, 19, 125
and herbs & flowers 18, 19, 35
and sprouts, leaves & roots 18, 79
suitable plants for 18, 19, 21
wheels, cucumbers on 148–53
whitefly 209
wilting 208
windowbox, fruit & flower 174–75

windowbox, scented geranium
& herb 42–45
windowsills, inside 17
windowsills, outside
growing Cape gooseberries 167
growing edible flowers 35, 42
growing fruit 167
growing fruiting vegetables on 16, 22, 125
growing herbs on 16, 22, 35, 42, 43
growing lettuce on 79
growing strawberries 167
wood chips 201
wooden planters 30

Z

zones, growing 16–23, 25
beneath skylights 16, 17, 18, 19, 35, 79, 95, 125, 167
best growing zones for fruit 167
best growing zones for fruiting vegetables 125
best growing zones for herbs & flowers 35
best growing zones for sprouts, leaves & roots 79
centre of a room 16, 20, 21, 35, 79, 125, 167
cool (unheated) south-facing room 16, 17, 22–23, 35, 79, 125, 167
dark corners 16, 20, 35, 79, 125, 167
east-facing windows 17, 18, 19, 35, 79, 125, 167
outside windowsill 16, 22, 35, 42, 43, 79, 125, 167
south-facing windows 16, 18, 19, 35, 79, 125, 167
walls 16, 20, 21, 35, 79, 125, 167
west-facing windows 16, 18, 19, 21, 35, 79, 125, 167

About the author

Author, book editor, and journalist, Zia Allaway is a qualified horticulturist and has written a range of gardening books for the RHS and DK, including ***The Complete Gardener's Manual, The Encyclopedia of Plants and Flowers, How to Grow Practically Everything***, and ***Growing Vegetables: 101 Essential Tips***. She has also worked with Diarmuid Gavin on two of his design books, and edited ***The Encyclopedia of Garden Design*** and the RHS Simple Steps series. Zia writes a monthly column on garden design for ***Homes & Gardens Magazine***, and is a contributor to the ***Garden Design Journal***. She runs a consultancy service from her home in Hertfordshire and offers practical workshops for beginners. She has a small wildlife garden which she opens to the public through the UK charity, The National Gardens Scheme.

Acknowledgements

This book has been a collaboration of words, design and photography and I would like to thank the whole team at DK for their dedication to the detail, with particular thanks to editor Susannah Steel for her editorial support and patience, stylist and designer Sonia Moore, who did an amazing job sourcing plants and props, and coordinating the growing of many crops, and photographer Will Heap who drove so many miles to take the beautiful images.

Thanks also to Angela Wilkes, managing editor Dawn Henderson for her critical eye, Alice Horne, designers Alison Gardner, Rehan Abdul, and Nicola Erdpresser who made this book look so amazing, Sarah Zadoorian for proofreading, and Vanessa Bird for the index.

Special thanks to Sally Harwood of Finchley Nurseries, who patiently grew and cared for many of the indoor plant projects, supported by owner George Coleman, and Sheila Clements and team at The Shaw Trust for caring for some of our plants and projects.

Thanks to Stephen and Serena Shirley of Victoriana Nurseries for the use of images and advice, Aylett Nurseries for the loan of plants and props, with special thanks to Kathy Sanger; Alexander Storch for his assistance with DIY projects; Alex Georgiou from Espresso Mushroom Company for his help and advice and wonderful oyster mushroom kits; Smithy's Mushrooms (smithymushrooms.co.uk) for donating products; Elho for their colourful containers; Ryan Bailey and team at Squires Garden Centre for the loan of plants and containers; Kezia from Conpot for the loan of concrete pots; Habitat for the loan of containers; and Suttons Seeds for some seeds and plants.

We are also indebted to Katie Khakpour-Smith, Susie Davidson, Rosslyn Perkins and Caroline Day-Lewis for the hire of their homes, and to Light Locations. Thanks also to Max Moore for prop and plant couriering and for his hands, which appear in most of the projects.

Last but not least, a huge thank you to my husband Brian North for his patience and support as I wrote this book, and my daughter Montana Allaway North for providing invaluable assistance at the photo shoots.

DISCLAIMER

Stevia (page 49) is used in many countries, including the US and Canada, to sweeten teas and other foods. EU legislation has yet to approve it as a culinary herb, but you can grow it as an ornamental if you do not wish to use it for culinary purposes.